Halki Diabetes Remedy

Eric Whitfield

CONTENTS

1   INTRODUCTION   1

2   THE PROTOCOL: THE HALKI DIABETES REMEDY   32

3   RECIPES   63

Readers are highly recommended to seek proper advice from either a physician or a professional practitioner before implementing any of these suggestions. Seriously, this book cannot replace professional and medical advice. Therefore, both the author and the publisher will not take any responsibility for any adverse results if readers really follow the information herein.

.

INTRODUCTION

Diabetes is everywhere these days. No one can hide from it anymore. It's common, misunderstood and the effects can be devastating.

As a researcher, my life for the past 20 plus years has been devoted to better understanding diabetes. I wanted answers. I wanted to help people, and I saw that in the world we live in, people just weren't being helped and more people were getting sick. Were people being treated? Absolutely. Turn on the TV and you'll see a new, 'improved' medication to deal with the condition. But are people really being helped to recover from their diabetes? With more and more people dying, more people developing diabetes, and getting the news that forever changes their lives, it really wouldn't seem so. Recovering from type 2 diabetes isn't something you hear of, or expect, and that just didn't feel right to me.

With my work I came across case after case of diabetes. I knew the stats and the studies, yet was missing the crucial information that would make everything come together. I knew everything about diabetes. I was aware of and had access to the cutting edge of research but was missing the solution.

You can imagine that after 20 years researching this condition I have come across my fair share of theories and further developments, as science continues to theorize on the causes of type 2 diabetes. Unfortunately, a consequence of this constantly changing research is the confusion it creates in people. Being told one thing one decade and something completely different the next, tends to confuse people, and more than this, it can destroy hope and makes people feel helpless.

When I met Eric Whitfield and his wife Cathy, it was one of those occasions in my career that truly felt like it was meant to be—and I'm not one for the idea of fate. However, that was how it felt, because they provided the missing piece of the puzzle. Not only did they provide the missing piece, but they reminded me of my initial reason for researching diabetes: the suffering. It was one thing for me to hide behind my academic textbooks and look at statistics, but experiencng the human, daily experience of diabetes is always humbling and serves as a reminder about why I do what I do and why getting the answer really matters. That was what Eric and Cathy gave me and I am forever grateful.

By the time I was introduced to Eric, he had already been through a lot. Caring for his wife, dealing with the financial strain and all the emotions that came with the entire heart-breaking experience, had understandably taken a toll. I could see the devastating effect that difficult time had on him, but I could also see his renewed sense of hope. It was only later that I understood why he had this hope, and I realized that if I had met him, even a few months earlier, that wouldn't have been the case. He had found the key so many of us have been looking for and it made the difference between watching his wife waste away and giving them their lives back.

Sadly, his experience is not rare. His story is one he shares with so many other people who have to watch their loved ones gradually deteriorate. And those people often don't have the same happy ending.

As I spoke to Eric, the more I knew he had stumbled across something incredible, and as I watched Cathy get stronger and stronger, until she was no longer even considered diabetic... that blew my mind. Suddenly it all added up, what I had been studying in the research for years and what I was seeing with my own eyes.

The Halki Diabetes Remedy was born and I knew it had the power to change the lives of millions.

The injustice of the whole thing finally melted away, people didn't have to suffer. Eric had found the solution I knew had to be out there. He told me about the people of Halki and the man who took him under his wing, Alexander Doukis, he showed me proof that the way these people live naturally makes diabetes impossible.

This eBook is my way of getting this vital information out into the world, and I am beyond excited to share this protocol with you. You don't need to be a prisoner to this disease and you definitely don't have to believe society when it tells you what life with diabetes is like. I mean, at one point humans believed the world was flat, right? Until someone proves the accepted norm is incorrect, everyone keeps believing a lie and that lie becomes the norm. But it's not normal, it's not how things have to be, and if you are someone who has resigned yourself to the idea that this is how life "just has to be," I want to be a voice that tells you it does not.

It means so much to me that I can write this eBook, that I can share with you information that has power to transform. It certainly transformed the lives of Eric and Cathy, regular people just like you, and I know they want other people to feel that same joy.

Amanda Feerson

YOU HAVE EVERYTHING YOU NEED

In a lot of health and self improvement books, you'll often find a section on how to achieve your goals. Goal setting is a major buzz word in the self improvement arena, and rightfully so. After all, what is the point of stuffing life-changing information in your head, if your new understanding

doesn't impact your actual life? Goals are a way to solidify what you want to achieve and how you

are going to get there; it helps translate head-knowledge to the material world around us. And isn't that what we all want? To have a better life, to be more fulfilled and happy? However, the kind of goal-setting I suggest here is a little different. I want you to achieve your goals, but I want more than this for you. Goals are great, but not when you feel bad when you don't meet your expectations, not when they become a source of discouragement, or another reason for you to be hard on yourself. So here are a few tips to make plans which inspire, instead of depress.

1) Focus on how you want to feel. Goals help you focus on an end point, on where you want to be. However, shifting your focus from a material outcome to an emotional one can help clarify what it is you really want. Then, in light of these feeling-based goals, you can ensure you are aiming yourself in the right direction. There's a saying I like, which highlights this point exactly: "You may get to the very top of the ladder, and then find it has not been leaning against the right wall." If you want your goals and planning to be effective, it's

important to do a little assessing before you begin; that is what helps you make sure you have indeed got 'the right wall.' SMART goals are great (in case you're not aware, SMART stands for Specific, Measurable, Achievable, Realistic and Time Bound) but for some people they can feel a bit claustrophobic to begin with. Start with how you want to feel, focus on the hope you can get from this book, and then look at setting some form of SMART goal. How do you set a feeling-based goal? I can presume that if you were to set a goal around your health it would be something like: I want to be diabetes-free in (amount of time.) That's an understandable goal. If you were to enquire about what you believe that goal will give you, what would you say? Are you seeking the peace of being diabetes-free? Security? Connection with loved ones? A renewed sense of purpose? Greater vitality? Really listen to what it is you want underneath the desire to live without diabetes. And, more than just how you want to feel, focus on what you will get from following the protocol and what it can give you. Focusing on the future, on what's possible, on what you want, can help get you unstuck and disengage from old, limiting beliefs. This gives you motivation!

2) Make peace with where you are. It's hard to be okay with where you are when it causes you suffering, but suffering more over the fact you're suffering, doesn't help much either! It's often easier to be okay with where we are when we know it won't last forever, and I (and

Eric, Cathy, Alexander, and the people of Halki) are here to give you that hope. Know that you are on your way to something great, know that you now have the information you need and that where you stand today will be the start-point of your success story. Knowing where you want to go is key, but making peace with where you are helps things from getting frustrating and helps you from burning out before you really get the chance to start. Remind yourself, again and again, that you are on your way and the pain you feel now, will be your joy later.

3) Know what you need to do. Don't fall into the trap of thinking you know it all. Plans often don't work because we don't follow them. It's really quite simple how we get off track— we don't remained focused on it. Remind yourself of what you need to include in your day, know exactly what ingredients you need to pick up from the store each week, make note of which ingredients are getting low and need to be replaced, know which dressings you'll be having that day and prepare them in advance if that's easier. It's easy to fool ourselves with the idea that things will just happen and work out on their own, but those kind of thoughts will only distract you for longer and stunt your progress. The longer you convince yourself that you know exactly what you need to do, while you don't and you're not doing what you need to.... yeah, that's how progress doesn't happen. Don't beat yourself up, but do make sure you know the protocol, take note of it, follow it and you will find success.

4) Go easy on yourself. Do what you need to do to make progress but don't be hard on yourself. We don't think of this when we think of goals, or moving forward, or self improvement, but it's important. We're too quick to judge, criticize and push ourselves, but chances are, pushing yourself is not what you need. Dealing with a health condition is already harsh enough, don't add your own expectations to the mix. It's highly likely you've been through the wringer in every way imaginable - mentally, emotionally, physically. You don't need additional pressure on yourself to be perfect. The protocol is designed to be simple and allow you to enjoy your life - keep it that way!

5) Switch off your brain. Your brain is useful when it comes to reading this eBook, making note of the instructions, amounts, planning etc, but when it comes to actually making progress, your

brain will not be your friend. Do what you can to switch it off in spare moments. Relax. Do meditation. Breathe deeply. Read your favorite book or listen to beautiful music. Do what you need to do to switch from doing, get-it-done, work mode to relaxation mode. Your body will thank you when you take the time to counteract the stress of the day. We all know stress isn't our friend, so make sure you don't turn this protocol into another source of stress. That's not what this is meant for. You can relax now. You have the information you need. You don't need to be worried about getting it right. If you're following the guidelines—if you know the ingredients you're picking up from the store, if you have the recipes and know which recipes you're following for the next couple of days—then you have

all you need. Then you can relax. Your body will know what to do with the precious substances you supply it and will do what it needs to self correct. Any stress on your part will simply stop the flow of healing.

6)   Plan ahead. Part of the success of any program is, quite simply, knowing what you need to do and knowing when things need to be done. In other words, it's just about being aware. There is little which needs to be changed in your life for the Halki Diabetes Remedy to work. The key is having the right ingredients in the house and ready to go, and always knowing the dressings and dips you're having that day. All that is required is some forethought, and that will make everything else run smoothly.

7)   Take things a day at a time. We need to plan ahead to make sure we're headed in the right direction, but it's also important to not get overwhelmed by the big picture and put energy into our here and now and the step we're on. Taking things a day at a time helps us do this. What would this look like on the 21 Day Plan? Look at the recipes for the week, make note of the shopping lists and what you

need to get from the store and then focus on the dips you're having that day and let the Diabetes Reversing 8 ingredients work their magic.

8)   Self care is an important aspect of health too. Your body has been through a lot. We're exposed to a lot of stress and environmental toxicity in this world, adding to it with your own thoughts doesn't make a lot of sense. Focus on ways that you can pamper yourself, soothe your emotions, calm your mind. Taking time out for yourself, regularly setting aside time to do things you love, and reconnecting who you really are can work wonders on your stress-level.

ISLAND OF WONDER

Until I met Eric, who told me of Alexander Doukis, I had never before heard of Halki. And when I started to learn about Halki, it made sense that I had never heard of it before. A tiny, small-populated Greek island in the Aegean Sea (and I do mean tiny, as of 2011 the census registered 478.) It is one of the smallest of the Dodecanese islands—only 11 square miles—and is, as you would expect: blue-skied, untainted, utterly beautiful, full of sunshine and warm people. It's hard to believe a place like that exists. But Halki is real and was known as, 'The Island of Peace and Friendship.' Quite the title.

Beyond it's inherent beauty, Halki houses another wonder. What I found on the island changed things forever and continues to change the lives of many. The island people, living their simple lives, hold onto a way of eating that is the key to ending diabetes. And the good news is you don't have to live on a paradisiacal Greek island to experience this (although if that were to happen that wouldn't be a bad thing, right?) The secrets of how these people lived are translatable to your life, wherever you are, and you don't need fancy, exotic ingredients that cost a fortune. The people on Halki live, what has been coined, the Mediterranean diet. This way of eating, a "centuries-old eating pattern"1, consists primarily of an abundance of fruit and vegetables, replacing butters and junk fats with healthy fats such as olive or canola oil, using nuts, whole grains and legumes, not having a diet heavy in red meat, and using a variety of herbs and spices. However, the lifestyle isn't one of deprivation, there is no fat-free or sugar-free anything—they don't skimp on the oil or wine—and yet they still exhibit long lifespans and a better quality of life. So much so, that in recent years this way of eating has garnered a fair amount of attention in the media, highlighting the benefits of this way of living and how other cultures can benefit from it too. Scientific studies have been performed to show how we can benefit from such a lifestyle and the difference it can make in our health. One such study, conducted in 2013, concluded that switching to this diet in midlife was "strongly linked to greater health and well-being in persons surviving to older ages."2 Two of the known benefits of eating this way comes from the amount of fiber—from the fruit, vegetables, legumes and whole grains—which are regularly consumed. Fiber helps slow digestion and control blood sugar. The second major benefit of this diet is the presence of monounsaturated fats found in oils, nuts and fish, that provide anti-inflammatory effects on the body.

The people of Halki have been living this way, and reaping the benefits for centuries, and only now is the rest of the world realizing the great potential of this way of eating. This is a fact even scientists can't ignore, announcing that, "The Mediterranean diet may be such a solution. It captures elements of both the TLC [Therapeutic Lifestyle Changes] and the DASH [Dietary Approaches to Stop

Hypertension] diets and provides more tangible recommendations (e.g., "Eat more fruits, and limit red meat" vs. "Limit intake of saturated fat to < 7% of overall calories"). Essentially, the Mediterranean diet, by design, affects blood glucose, blood pressure, and cholesterol management, making it an intriguing choice for diabetes clinicians and their patients."3

It just goes to show how ahead of the curve the people of Halki have been! And thankfully, we Americans don't have to do an overhaul on our current way of living to reap the benefits of the Mediterranean diet, we just have to know exactly what makes their diet so powerful and transfer those exact components to our diet. This is what Eric Whitfield discovered and shared with me, and this is what you will learn as you keep reading.

NOT JUST ANOTHER EBOOK

I don't know your history, how long your life has been affected by diabetes, if you're reading this to treat yourself or someone you know who you desperately want to help. I don't know the specifics of your life, but since I have spent the last 20 years absorbed in the world of diabetes, researching the condition and learning as much as I can, I know how powerless the disease can make you feel.

This may be your first attempt to do something outside of what your doctor recommends in their office. This may be the first time you've felt able to take your health into your own hands and do something yourself, or you may have picked up this starter guide as a last resort after suffering with diabetes for decades and you simply don't know what else to do. If that's the case, you may have started this eBook feeling you know all there is to know, you may be at the end of your rope and feeling pretty jaded. All of those emotions are understandable. And all of those emotions will be an asset to you when it comes to creating change, because change doesn't come from a half-hearted person, change comes to those who really want it and my guess is you really want it or you wouldn't have started this eBook. Those emotions will be your motivation to create a better life for yourself, and I'll tell you a secret, that better life—a diabetes free life—is just around the corner. No kidding. So if you do feel worn out, or jaded, or overwhelmed and exasperated, or all of the above, you won't be feeling that way for long.

This is a fresh start. Anything you may have tried before discovering this protocol, doesn't matter. You may have read books, and been told statistics and dooming facts by your doctor. You may have already tried different diets and health plans, numerous medications and treatments (there certainly isn't a shortage of any of those.)

Chances are, you know a lot of information about diabetes. After months and years of dealing with it and defining yourself by it, how could you not? I know you must be really tired of the whole thing. That's why this eBook won't focus on what you already know, the same old stuff that keeps you locked in the past, the usual data you've heard a million times before. You want a new way: a dynamic, profound, life-altering method. This is what this eBook offers. We won't fill your head with facts that any Google search will bring up.

The aim of this material is to help show you that you have found the answer. No more searching is required. This is it.

Quite the promise, huh?

Keep reading and learning more about the Halki Diabetes Remedy and you will understand how I can make such a claim. After seeing the effects of this cure in the lives of suffering people, people just like you, there is no doubt in my mind or hesitation as I write those words. I know the power of this remedy and it is a joy to share the solution with you, to know this information is what people have been endlessly searching for, praying for, but unable to find. So whatever your

personal circumstance with diabetes, if you're reading this for someone else, reading it for yourself, considered to have prediabetes, already a diabetic or just looking at creating a preventative lifestyle, this is the book for you, a source of assurance that you're on the right path and you are never powerless.

THE POWER OF ADDITION

We have some pretty set ideas when it comes to health. We see healthy people as being those who go out for 20 mile runs, have less than 5% body fat, drink glasses of green juice with extra kale, never smoke, drink, eat sugar.... in other words, they're perfect. Of course when compared with this standard a good 95% of us would fall short. In fact, most of us would conclude that if that's what it takes to be healthy, it really doesn't seem like a lot of fun. And isn't life supposed to be enjoyed?

This is extremist thinking and it stops us from ever really getting anywhere or even making a start.

I am here to tell you that you don't need to be a jogging, green-juice-drinking fanatic, or turn into one, to make a change to your health. That's the amazing thing, and it's also the heartbreaking thing when it comes to people who are already suffering from disease. It doesn't have to be that way and it doesn't take what people think it will take to make positive steps forward. They don't need to turn into someone else, someone they've never been, someone who is perfect and never enjoys their food again.

THIS IS THE INCREDIBLE NEWS!

If you have been stopped in the past from making changes, thinking you'll never have what it takes, that you're not   (fill in the blank) enough, that's a lie. You don't have to be someone else to make this protocol work. You get to be yourself and work from where you are and see incredible things happen as a result.

This is done through something a lot of people overlook: simply adding things to what you already do.

As human beings, so often, we focus on taking things away. We tell ourselves that in order to be healthy we must deprive ourselves. Just look at all the diets marketed on the planet. And sure, there are some that say you can still have ice cream or cookies after dinner, but it always comes with a catch; they're still focusing on the idea of depriving yourself of what you want. You still have to adhere to the calorie limit, or count the carbs, or leave out the cheese (whatever the case may be.)

And we're not good at this as human beings. Our minds go a little crazy at the thought of what we love being taken from us. Just imagine a 5 year old who suddenly has their beloved snow cone or corndog stolen from them as they are about to bite in... are they happy? In reality, we never really grow out of that response. We can tell ourselves that we really don't need the extra slice of pie, but there's a part of us that still wants it.

Now, am I saying we should eat whatever we want, all the time, regardless of the cost? No.

What I am saying, is that we miss one of the most powerful methods for creating change

when we don't look at what we can add to what we already do.

This is how we create momentum.

Create success by adding things in while you keep doing all that you already do.

This may challenge all you've ever been told about what it takes to improve your health. Let's not overlook the fact that it would be great if we could snap our fingers and become the kind of person who would never want to do anything ever again which would jeopardize their health, but let's be realistic, is that ever going to happen? Has it worked for you so far? Most people need to start slow, not try to be something they're not, because we've all tried to make New Years resolutions—or seen people who have made resolutions—and then burn out spectacularly 2 weeks later. This is often too extreme for us; too much, too fast. We get to Z, when we go through the other 25 letters. One step at a time. But this is not what we often do, we start at A and expect to fast-forward to W or X. It's a seductive idea, that we can wake up one day and reject the way we've been living for the last couple of decades (or our whole lives,) and by sheer willpower, determination and the force of our spirit, break the chains of our habits. This is not reality. Willpower and determination are great things, but we build on them as we go, as we gain that momentum and make progress. At the beginning, we often don't have enough and this is when we burn out.

We have certain idealized fantasies about changing out lives, and they tend to emphasize this extreme A to Z transition. And while the dream of that is nice and inspiring—it sells tickets to motivational speaking seminars and get us all pumped up—for most of us it doesn't work. We're in too deep, real life gets in the way, negative thoughts pop up, stuff happens. That is not a sign that you can't do it, it's just information that it may need to be done another way. And let's face it, when you're worn down from years of struggling with disease and feeling powerless, how much energy do you think you really have to spend on harsh, extreme changes? You're barely surviving the week and you want to heap unrealistic expectations and a rigid dietary schedule on yourself?

So drop all of those pressures and expectations. Drop however you may have tried things in the past, what you think is possible and how you believe change happens. All you have to do is start. Don't even attempt to remove anything from the way you live or force yourself to be someone else. Believe that if you take certain steps, if you add the right things, the natural

consequence is progression. Change is automatic if you add the right things to your life. Let that sink in. Change. Is. Automatic. You don't even have to try. Do you need to focus on not floating off the ground? No, gravity takes care of that. Forget to tell your heart to keep beating and have it stop for a whole 7 minutes before you remember and get it going again? Mmm, I'm guessing not. Yet we treat ourselves like this all the time when it comes to making positive changes to our health. We think we need to micromanage every second of the day and force ourselves to act like that new, artificially enforced person every second of the 24 hour day and wonder why we can't sustain such an act.

This isn't about forcing yourself to be someone you're not. You naturally become who you are meant to be by choosing your first step wisely. If you choose wisely, the rest happens as a consequence of that one thing.

Choosing wisely. That's key.

That's what this protocol is for; the Diabetes Reversing 8, those are wise choices. You're not throwing random supplements at yourself and hoping for the best, you're not living on carrots for a month and burning out after 5 days and vowing to never touch a carrot again. You are taking charge of your health by knowing what will have the most impact and doing that one thing over and over again.

See, wise...

And it's doable. It's achievable. It is mere steps away from where you are and that means better health is just round the corner, not for some green juice drinking 20 year old, but for you.

This is how change happens. One step at a time. This is how you become diabetes-free. Add the right things and watch the magic happen.

TOXICITY

The Greek philosopher Hippocrates, acknowledged as the 'Father of Medicine,' is well known for saying: "Let food be thy medicine." Despite the fact he was born in 460 BC, there has never been a time when these words have not had relevancy, and in actual fact, they may be more relevant in our day and age, which is rampant with lifestyle-controlled disease. Our modern-day dietary advice tends to reduce food to carbohydrates, proteins, fats and calories. Yet, If we were to look deeper, hiding behind this masquerade, is something else and it is that 'something else' which will make all the difference when it comes to your health. A carrot isn't good to eat because it's low in calories or fat, but because of what it contains: phytonutrients. This is what will really make you healthy. We need these protective, detoxifying, restorative phytonutrients. That's why you won't be counting a single calorie with the Halki Diabetes Remedy (that would actually be a complete

waste of time.) What you will be doing is including vegetables and substances which give your body what it really needs to heal. That is the difference of this protocol. The Diabetes Reversing 8, which you will be introduced to in the upcoming sections, will be what makes the difference between your life with diabetes and your diabetes-free life. No exaggeration. And so, as I introduce you to these powerhouse substances I want you to really take note. They are chosen because of science, because of their potency, their potential and power when they interact with your body. No one is less than the other and they all deserve the spotlight in your mission of reclaiming your health.

One of the reasons we need the protective power of the Diabetes Reversing 8 is to help our body deal with toxicity, the toxins which are all around us and which our body is exposed to every day. The great news is, that despite the fact we're exposed to these toxins, our body has the innate power to heal. Long before our modern-day health system, there was the belief that our body was able to heal itself. Now this doesn't mean it was believed human beings could regenerate a lost limb like a chameleon—that is not the kind of healing they spoke of—the kind of healing our forefathers believed in, was the body's ability to self-regulate and self-correct. Just think about it, what happens when you get a cold? Slice your finger when chopping a tomato? What does your body do? Your body has an innate self-healing mechanism designed to keep you healthy. We accept these small healing moments as normal and nothing to get excited about, yet think about what your body is actually doing... really think about it. It's no small thing. Your body does this all the time, in ways you don't even think about. In fact, while you are reading this, your body is managing numerous processes in order to sustain your life in the best way it can.

I can hear some of you thinking: "But my body hurts. It's made me suffer for years and given me numerous issues. It's really trying to help me? Can you tell it to do a better job?" When your body has felt like an enemy for years, when it has become the source of your emotional/mental/ physical/financial pain, it is completely understandable that your appreciation and ability to see what your body is capable of has been crushed.

However, think back to when you were 5. Did you have to will your grazed knee to heal? What about your broken bone from falling off the swing or your nose bleed? You thought nothing of those things when you were young, your body just dealt with it. The only difference is—not your age—but the toxic accumulation that has occurred between the 5 year old You and the You of today. You are not old and decrepit, you have just been exposed to many different harmful substances during your lifetime. Those toxins affect how efficiently your body can work, and in your case, how well it can deal with longer term conditions like diabetes. In the upcoming sections you will discover more about this toxic accumulation, as well as how these toxins cause your ill health.

The Halki Diabetes Remedy deals with these toxins, and that is why this isn't a doomed situation. I am telling you all of this since there is a solution. You can give your body the help it needs to kick it's innate healing ability back into gear.

Drum roll please.

It's about to get exciting.

SOMETHING JUST DOESN'T ADD UP

As a society we're used to repeating "2+2=5" and seeing nothing wrong with the answer. We don't recognize that we're repeating a lie, something which is completely incorrect, and this stops us from examining the original calculation.

There are times when it's important to make sure things still add up. If we base our lives on lies, everything that comes from that base will likewise be affected and distorted, and if you really want positive, true change, the lies needs to be pulled out. In order for you to get the life you seek, the health you so deeply desire, the relief from the health-related suffering you experience, we need to address our inaccurate conclusions, because those beliefs won't get you where you want to go. If you alter the flight coordinates on a plane by only a couple of degrees, that difference will take you away from your intended destination, and it's the same in our lives, those few degrees take us off-track. It's important to get the calculation right in order to get to where you want to go. Let's correct our "coordinates." That is the purpose of this section.

What are the 5's that we, and our society, are telling us about diabetes?

We live in a time where we have access to scientific information, advanced healthcare, gyms that are open 24 hours a day, organic foods in our grocery stores, awareness of what diabetes is and how we should treat it (even if that understanding is ultimately wrong,) doctors who can administer the latest medications and treatments.... so why is diabetes still such an issue? Why does it seem to be everywhere and developing in people who seem the most unlikely to harbor it? Why is it the epidemic that it is?

This is what doesn't add up. With all these advances, with the knowledge, with our access to health-promoting things, why is nothing changing and why is it actually getting worse?

$2+2=5$

Since such a large proportion of the population is developing type 2 diabetes, we're starting to accept this as the new norm. But things didn't used to be this way. So what has changed? Why are we accepting something without fully examining the facts?

This is the mission of this ebook. I've done the academic, research-based footwork so you can just focus on doing what it takes to change your health, on your own, without the almighty help of a medical institution. Accurate knowledge and yourself are the only things you need for your diabetes to be completely reversed!

I would encourage you to discard everything you thought you knew about diabetes and start over. You don't need the old information and assumptions. If you have trouble doing this I would suggest you do 2 things: 1) reflect on how your current and past assumptions have helped your diabetes so far and 2) try the protocol and see the results for yourself.

Over the next few sections you will be presented with the key contributors to type 2 diabetes, the real reasons diabetes is such an epidemic. You will be shown information that concludes 2+2=4. No more accepting rationales that don't match the reality. You will be able to see why the discrepancies and inconsistencies we see in the world are attributed to the wrong things. Everything will start to make so much more sense, everything will add up. Finally.

AIR: THE REAL KILLER

We are waking up to the true cost of air pollution. It has been one of those subjects which has been far too easy to just sweep under the rug and pretend it's not there. We can't do this anymore, too much is at stake, too much evidence is pilling up warning us of what is really happening, there is too much damage being caused to be content with denial. The alternative of waking up, of staying stuck in denial instead, is killing us.

Denial makes us believe nothing is wrong. Denial tells us that if things were really bad, the 'top dogs' in the country—the people in positions of power who are aware of potential dangers— would do what it takes to keep us safe. However, this isn't the case and it's not what the evidence shows. More and more studies and statistics are emerging which show the prevalence of air pollution and the deadly effect it has on our health. In fact, we now know that "there is no safe air pollution level at which adverse health effects are absent."4 In the past, we were aware of how pollution negatively impacts the environment. Well, when you walk around in the world, your body becomes part of the environment too. Yet somehow we tended to overlook this. Bottom line: if you live and breathe on this planet, you are being exposed to that deadly pollution. Just this year, the Committee on the Medical Effects of Air pollutants (COMEAP), took the various studies performed over the last decade and concluded that pollution caused cardiovascular inflammation, altered the heart's normal rhythm, increased the probability of blood clots, increased blood pressure and the build-up of fatty material inside the arteries. Combine this with the World Health Organization (WHO), announcing that air pollution is 'the new tobacco'5, and the evidence is clear: air pollution is killing us, and in great numbers. The new stats show it is responsible for the deaths of 7 million people each year and damaging the health of billions more across the globe.

This comparison to smoking is a poignant one. Over the past few decades, due to our increasing knowledge about the cost of smoking, our attitude to this once-considered harmless, recreational habit no longer holds. And now, we have a society which has taken appropriate measures to contain the damage of smoking, to help protect people, since we realized it wasn't just the people smoking the cigarette who damaged their health, people who didn't even put the cigarette to their lips, were also harmed. This was termed third-hand smoking. A person didn't have to smoke, they didn't even have to inhale the smoke willingly and knowingly, a person could be harmed just by being around an extinguished tobacco product. The same is true for pollution. We may not put the pieces together ourselves— how pollution is really influencing our bodies— since we don't necessarily see pollution as easily as a cigarette hanging out of someone's mouth, but the damage is being done without us knowing. Smoking is nothing compared to a danger which is everywhere and which we haven't even known is happening. This needs to be the next shift in our health awareness. Smoking, something which once seemed so normal, was discovered for what it really is: a killer. The same is happening around the issue of air pollution. It is, as Dr Tedros Adhanom Ghebreyesus, the WHO's director general, announced, "a silent public health emergency."6

This is bad enough for an adult, but for the rising generation, for young children and infants, this impact compounds. There are even worries about what this means for pregnant women and their unborn children, since exposure to this fine particulate matter has been linked to birth defects.7 Exposure is exposure, even if it's in the womb.

We have to wake up.

The deadliest type of air pollution is PM2.5 (the 'P.M.' stands for particulate matter.) This type of pollution is composed of particles that are small enough to slip by the body's defenses and bury themselves deep in the lungs, even entering the bloodstream. This is one of the reasons they are so deadly, "the smaller these particles are, the more damage they can wreak on the human body."8 This information alone can explain how air pollution and diabetes are linked. If these tiny particles are able to invade our body in such a way, there is no end to how insulin production and sensitivity would

be effected. To help you envision how small these particles really are, they are described as being "30 times smaller than the width of a human hair."9 Pretty tiny... and worse still, these tiny particles have been linked to the development of both short and long-term health conditions, creating health related issues days or even hours after exposure. When you think about it, this would make perfect sense.

How could breathing in tiny, deadly air particles not affect our body?

And affect us it does, since in 2015 it was found that "ambient pm 2.5 was the fifth-ranking mortality risk factor... [causing] 4.2 milliton deaths and 103.1 million disability-

adjusted life-years"10 And sadly, the numbers are only rising. Just in the 3 years since that

statement was made, things are getting increasingly worse.

It may be hard to accept that things are that bad in a nation like ours, in the United States, however, once you understand the nature of PM 2.5 as well as how the sources of PM 2.5 are integrated into our 'normal lives,' you'll begin to see how things can be that bad without us being any the wiser.

To explore our 'cultural blindness' deeper, it's crucial to understand how PM 2.5 operates and how this makes it so dangerous. As already explained, '2.5' refers to the particle size. The particle- size effects how the particle behaves. Generally, the smaller the particle, the more it's ability to "remain airborne for long periods and travel hundreds of miles."11 That's one of the main reasons you can't count living in a remote village, far from civilization, as protection from the deadly influence of these particles. Just by their very nature, they are not localized or contained, but spread easily and stay in the air for long periods of time. You can't escape the deadly influence, no matter where you live.

Secondly, the sources of such damaging pollution are all around us and woven into the fabric of our daily lives. Natural sources of PM 2.5 aren't the issue, since they contribute such a small amount to the overall problem. What generates this unhealthy level of particulate matter is us and the way we live. Cars, for example, are a common source of PM 2.5 and whilst we know this is the case—that cars are a source of pollution—that is not something we have personalized yet to our own wellbeing. Yet, the reality is that right in our driveway is a source of something which is harming millions of people. Other sources of PM 2.5, besides vehicles, are "classified according to six different sources: electric power generation, industry, commercial and residential sources, road transportation, marine transportation and rail transportation."12

To give this more weight, the World Health Organization (WHO) announced that 80% of the world's population lives in areas which exceed the 'air quality guideline' (AQG), a guideline which was established for human wellbeing. In fact, some regions have an air quality with PM 2.5 concentrations which exceed the AQG several times over, and yet it is known that: "Reduction in exposure [to PM 2.5] will yield substantial health benefits."13 This offers a concrete explanation for our declining health as a nation. However, the average person walking around doesn't know about this, let alone think to correlate this situation with their health because they can't even see the problem! Have you ever looked at the sky and said, "oh look, there's some PM 2.5!" No! We don't even identify the danger, we don't know that being in the big wide world and breathing is correlated to the health issues we suffer from. Why would we? Even if we do experience any temporary issues from breathing in this toxic matter, often the experience is so short-lived, it ends and we go about our day none the wiser and attribute it to or 'allergies' or last night's meal, and we certainly don't link that short-lived experience to something we think is totally unrelated like air pollution.

Another consequence of air pollution is the oxidative stress it creates in the body. Oxidative stress is, essentially, when the equilibrium between free radicals and anti-oxidants within the body become imbalanced, with free radicals outnumbering the anti-oxidants. Think of leaving a cut apple out in the open. At first, the apple is as it should be, vibrant, clean-looking and fresh. However, leave it out on the side for 30 minutes—or even 10—and you will see the effect of oxidation. While we are not apples, that visual comparison can help you picture how oxidation results in damage and degeneration. An abundance of oxidation in the body does more than you would witness with a left-out apple, it leads to disease, to the "oxidative damage [of] biomolecules, (lipids, proteins, DNA), eventually leading to many chronic diseases such as atherosclerosis, cancer, diabetes, rheumatoid arthritis, post-ischemic perfusion injury, myocardial infarction, cardiovascular diseases, chronic inflammation, stroke and septic shock, ageing and other degenerative diseases."14

Once you realize oxidative stress is capable of such destruction in your body, it's easy to wonder how it has personally affected you.

How is the toxicity you're surrounded by every day affecting you? How has it played a part in the acquisition and development of diabetes? Based on science, it has everything to do with the current state of your physical health and the development of type 2 diabetes. It is responsible for it all.

And yet sadly, we've been pointing the finger in the wrong direction. When we think of diabetes, we don't create this correlation on our own—that "the global toll of diabetes attributable to PM 2.5 air pollution is significant"[15]—we still run on the belief that type 2 diabetes occurs as the result of being overweight and eating too many sugary, fatty foods. And if we believe this rationale, it's easy to think that type 2 diabetes is something for which we should be punished. After all, when following that popular belief, we think that the condition is something developed because of us, because of something we did. We blame ourselves. You might be one of the many people who believe you brought diabetes on yourself, however our new understanding, and the scientific evidence, all points in the same direction, to the same conclusion: type 2 diabetes develops because of large-scale environmental factors, factors that aren't even in your control!

And the truth is, even researchers are spotting huge flaws in our beliefs about diabetes. As Atul Butte, MD, PhD, associate professor of systems medicine in paediatrics, said, "While plenty of genetic risk factors for type-2 diabetes have been found... none of them taken alone, and not even all of them taken together, comes close to accounting for the prevalence of type-2 diabetes."[16] There is something we're not taking into account. Like the previous quotation shows, genetics don't account for the epidemic of diabetes. But what does account for this epidemic is the particulate matter in our air which "contribute[s] to around 3.2 million cases of diabetes and the loss of 8.2 million years of healthy life in 2016."17 We are finally understanding what's really to blame for this wide-spread problem, and the deadly cycle it keeps us stuck in: exposure to PM 2.5, oxidative stress and the topic we'll talk about next, inflammation. It really is an epidemic, one that only worsens with time, and is predicted to keep worsening from year to year.

You might live out in the beautiful, unspoilt countryside, barely see a car or notice any kind of pollution. Surely, this whole PM 2.5 thing is overreacting for someone in my location, you may be thinking.

Trouble is, none of us are immune, none of us can escape the effects of PM 2.5, no matter where you live. This is a global problem, and while it can be easy to push an issue like this 'outside of you' to other places and countries. This is happening, literally, in our own back yard. In your back yard, in your neighbours back yard, down the road, in the next county, in the next state. This is a global problem. One we all face and one where hiding, doesn't help. Telling yourself there's no weeds in your back yard doesn't get rid of the weeds, right? Likewise, pretending that air quality isn't an issue or a key contributor to your declining health, won't help you. Evidence shows otherwise.

What will help, and make all the difference, is taking the information which is on this page and using it to your advantage. There are things that can be done to protect you from further attack as well as correct the damage that has already been done.

This may have been a lot for you to assimilate. This may be the first time you've heard the extent of the problem, and it is truly a catastrophic problem which looms over us, but knowledge is power and now we do know what is really going on, it would be unwise for us to ignore this information. Being scared doesn't help, but using this knowledge to empower yourself and how you live your life, so you can be in control, be informed and wise in the decisions you make, is the best thing you can do. I will restate the opening of this section: we are waking up to the cost of air pollution. Waking up is the key, because once that happens we can do something. And this eBook is all about doing something.

THE IMPACT OF INFLAMMATION

Inflammation is a natural and necessary part of your body's defense system which is activated when there's an injury. It helps protect you, signalling to the immune system where there needs to be healing and physiological issues which need to be addressed. However, when there is chronic and prolonged inflammation, this helpful, protective process can cause some pretty devastating effects.

There are two kinds of inflammation—acute and chronic. Acute is the kind which occurs when you graze your knee or get a sore throat. The body usually deals with this kind of inflammation within a short period of time and the inflammation resolves. Chronic inflammation, on the other hand, is long-term and far reaching in it's effects. Unlike the localized inflammation that comes from something like a cut, chronic inflammation gets worse over time and doesn't self-correct or allow the body can get on with the job of healing. Chronic inflammation interferes with this healthy process.

Another problem arises when the body produces chronic inflammation to a perceived threat, overreacting to nothing and depleting the body. An oversensitized, easily triggered system will continuously activate the inflammation response, creating a cycle which can be hard to break. This kind of chronic inflammation has been compared to a slow-burning fire which will, in time, attack even the healthy areas in our body.

Inflammation is linked to the development of major disease—

autoimmune disorders, heart disease, stroke and even cancer. In fact, the National Cancer Institute has announced that "chronic inflammation can cause DNA damage and lead to some forms of cancer."18 Without the understanding that this information gives us, it's easy to see why we point the finger in all the wrong directions and enter a worsening cycle of health: because we don't even know what created the cycle in the first place!

Thankfully, we are discovering more about the real cause of diseases with every passing year. Whereas before, we would never think to connect these things together, now we see how it's all interconnected. Such extreme, life-threatening illness is being traced back to it's actual catalyst, and in the case of type 2 diabetes and inflammation, we are finding more that, "subclinical inflammation may be [the] mechanism linking air pollution with type 2 diabetes."19

So other than when you get a bump, or cut, or sore throat, what causes inflammation? "A growing body of evidence has implicated inflammatory responses to ... environmental factors as a key mechanism that help explain the emerging epidemic in diabetes."20 That's right, the focus comes back to the environmental influence when it comes to our health. Whether it's oxidative stress, inflammation, free radicals and on and on... they can all be traced back to the effect our environment is having on us.

If these environmental factors can so severely affect our body, and even contribute or cause serious diseases like cancer, that's a pretty major thing. Fortunately, there are things we can do, which are within our realm of control—one of the main ones being our lifestyle choices. Foods are commonly known to affect inflammatory reactions and are therefore one of the things we can use to effect our bodies. That's right, there are anti-inflammatory foods, foods which will actually help inflammation and positively impact your health:

"...the intake of anti-oxidant and anti- inflammatory nutrients... ameliorate various respiratory and cardiovascular effects of air pollution through reductions in oxidative stress and inflammation."21 You can experience all kinds of benefits when you make wise, strategic choices around your lifestyle. Research shows this more and more.

To most people this information is a lot to process, since there is a lot of information out there which makes us think these major diseases are merely random chance, or due to our inherited genetics, but what we often overlook, the information we don't have, is what will make the biggest difference. You don't have to be a victim to chronic disease, you don't even have to be a victim to inflammation! That's the amazing thing! That's why I am so excited to get this book out into the world! You can treat your disease. You can treat diabetes. You can treat inflammation, It is in your hands! Are you starting to feel excited?

IT'S NOT JUST DIABETES...

Here we are, wrapping things up for this entire section. By this point you understand the power of inflammation and its role in disease, you've read how one source of this inflammation is caused by environmental stressors like pollution and how this creates inflammation and why this all matters. Alongside this health conundrum however, I have also outlined why this isn't a futile situation and how all this information will help you create a beautiful new story for yourself.

With the knowledge and power which is loaded in this protocol, the one you will be introduced to on the following pages, you will see how diabetes can be reversed. This is hard science. Fact. The studies upholding the protocol, the Halki Diabetes Remedy, show how all these components come together to bring about change in your body.

Are you ready for what this protocol will give you? This isn't just another diet plan, like one of the many you may have tried in your life, it is based on scientific discovery and profound understanding on how to treat diseases. Yes, I said 'diseases', since, "Many doctors and research scientists now believe that most chronic diseases may have the same root cause: inflammation."22 Addressing a root cause is the only real way to address a problem, in fact it's the only way to permanently address it. No more masking the symptoms or going after the wrong thing, no more wasting time or burning out. The Halki Diabetes Remedy addresses the root of the problem once and for all: strengthening the body as a whole, fortifying your entire system, and addressing the underlying chronic inflammation and toxicity—everything that is keeping you sick. You will finally be able to allow your body to do what it naturally does: heal, come back to balance and equilibrium. Do you see how different this is from what you've been told before?

With an approach like this, type 2 diabetes will not be the only positive change in your health. By simply introducing the knowledge from the protocol, you are about to impact your body in all sorts of ways. Diabetes isn't the only thing which will be addressed by the protocol. Are you ready to change everything about your health? Then read on...

THE PROTOCOL: THE HALKI DIABETES REMEDY

A study conducted in 2015 on the 'Nutritional Solutions to Reduce Risks of Negative Health Impacts of Air Pollution', stated: "While reducing levels [of air pollution] is the ultimate goal, achieving sustainable reductions that fully protect the population, is not likely

to occur in the foreseeable future...the most effective and wide

reaching interventions... likely operate along common inflammatory and oxidative stress pathways... Interventions, which may ameliorate

inflammatory effects or oxidative stress, may be among the most widely applicable." The

conclusion drawn? Address issues of oxidative stress and inflammation through the diet, specifically through the addition of certain substances. Unlike the medications which are used to 'treat' diabetes, which only mask the symptoms and don't address the real cause, this protocol goes straight to the heart of the matter, addressing the real issues so permanent change is achieved. The protocol you will learn about in the following sections will do this through "anti- oxidant and anti-inflammatory nutrients," incorporating as many of these healing foods as possible.

By now, I'm sure you're eager to get to the information about these life-changing substances

—the Diabetes Reversing 8—and because of that, I'm going to cut this introduction short and get right to it...

INTRODUCING THE DIABETES REVERSING 8

The Diabetes Reversing 8 are the heart of the Halki Diabetes Remedy. They will give your body exactly what it needs to combat type 2 diabetes. In this section you will be introduced to each of the 8 diabetes reversing substances, you will discover why they are so fundamental to this protocol and what they will do for you. You may, or may not, have heard of them. If you have and are underestimating their power, just wait till the end of this section and I know you will feel differently.

1. Glucoraphanin

2. Sulforaphane

3. Vitamin C

4. Vitamin E

5. β-Carotene

6. Omega-3 fatty acid

7. Ginger

8. Magnesium

1.   Glucoraphanin

Chances are you haven't heard of Glucoraphanin. Glucoraphanin is a potent antioxidant, it is the precursor to sulforaphane and belongs to a group of compounds called glucosinolates, which are found in cruciferous vegetables.25 The health benefits which come from these compounds are numerous, well-documented and definitely not to be overlooked. Just recently in 2015 it was found that, "consumption of high glucoraphanin broccoli significantly reduces plasma LDL-C."26 An additional bonus for those with high cholesterol.

2.   Sulforaphane

After glucoraphanin is converted it becomes another compound, sulforaphane, a compound reputed for it's "tumor prevention properties."27 It is a major phytochemical found in cruciferous foods like broccoli, brussel sprouts, bok choy, cabbage, cauliflower, collards, chinese broccoli, kale, mustard, radish, arugula, and watercress.28 These compounds (both Glucoraphanin and sulforaphane) are key players to good health, providing anti-cancer properties,29 decreasing cell damage, and "reduc[ing] the inflammatory effects of oxidative stress."30 Concerning diabetes, this compound has been found to address, "exaggerated glucose production and glucose intolerance... [it also] reduced fasting blood glucose and glycated hemoglobin."31

MYROSINASE: THE UNSUNG HERO

While not part of the Diabetes Reversing 8, myrosinase is another piece of the puzzle when it comes to sulforaphane, and as such, requires mentioning. Myrosinase, an enzyme found in broccoli, is key for sulforaphane to form. However, in order to ensure myrosinase is utilized and not destroyed, it can be paired with another myrosinase-rich food, then between the two, sulforaphane can be restored. This

is explained by Elizabeth Jeffrey, PhD, researcher at University of Illinois, "Mustard, radish, arugula, wasabi and other uncooked cruciferous vegetables such as cole slaw all contain myrosinase, and we've seen this can restore the formation of sulforaphane."[32]

3. Vitamin C

Also known as ascorbic acid, vitamin c acts as an anti-oxidant. Similar to other anti-oxidants in this list, vitamin C combats free radicals which are present in the body. It's very common for people to mention this vitamin when they have a cold and want to give their immune system a boost, and this is for good reason since, "healthier levels of vitamin C can enhance immune function, reduce inflammatory conditions such as atherosclerosis, and significantly lower blood pressure. But even beyond this, it benefits collagen production, wound healing, and the

absorption of iron. Interestingly, vitamin C has also been discovered to "completely prevent"[34] airway hyper-responsiveness, improving the respiratory system's ability to deal with airborne pollutants. This isn't the only study which highlights vitamin C's crucial role in helping the body deal with air pollutants, many more studies are confirming this fact with each passing year. The main benefit of an anti-oxidant like vitamin C, is the effect it has on free radicals, helping to readdress the improper balance, leading to better health and vitality.

4.   Vitamin E

Providing anti-oxidant properties which can protect cell degeneration, vitamin E fights inflammation35, promotes good immune function and combats free radicals. In fact, Harvard's school of public health announced that, "vitamin E supplementation was linked to a 24 percent lower risk of cardiovascular death. And among women ages 65 and older, vitamin E supplementation reduced the risk of major cardiac events by 26 percent. A later analysis found that women who took the vitamin E supplements also had a lower risk of developing serious blood clots in the legs and lungs, with women at the highest risk of such blood clots receiving the greatest benefit." When this anti-oxidant was studied for it's ability to help asthmatics who were exposed to air pollutants, it was concluded that both vitamin E and C helped the lungs function and perform better, even when under stress.36 With amazing outcomes like this, vitamin E plays an important part in restoring health.

5.   β-Carotene

The precursor to Vitamin A, β-Carotene—also known as beta carotene—is an anti-oxidant that helps promote healthy skin, teeth, mucus membranes, and vision. Beta carotene is what gives fruits and vegetables their yellow/orange color, but is also found is vegetables which are not yellow/orange (like peas, spinach and onions.) When concerning diabetes, the British Medical Journal's Open Diabetes Research announced that, "consumption of carotenoids, especially pro- vitamin A carotenoids, could reduce the risk of type 2 diabetes"37 and reinforcing this belief is another study which states,

"Vitamin A and related synthetic retinoids could be new drugs for the treatment of diabetes."38 By obtaining beta carotene through the diet, and not supplementation, there is the added bonus that the body uses only what it needs and then discards the rest. This is an advantage over taking supplements, since any unwanted vitamin A taken through a supplement would be stored in fatty tissue and accumulate. Not so when it is received through dietary means. Dietary vitamin sources are better than supplementation - another reason why our dressings pack such a punch!

6. Omega 3 Fatty Acid

Suggested as having profound anti-inflammatory properties, Omega 3 Fatty Acids, positively influence a number of systems in the body, as well as helping the brain properly function. With diabetes, Omega 3 is known to reduce insulin resistance by increasing adiponectin (a hormone) and lowering triglyceride levels, helping prevent any future heart disease. Specifically, when considering the effects of PM2.5 air pollution, scientific studies have concluded that Omega 3 "appeared to blunt the adverse changes ... with increased PM2.5 and black carbon concentrations."39 And just taking 2 grams a day of fish oil "prevented HRV [heart rate variability] related to PM 2.3 exposure."40 Other studies of this precious oil have shown how it can help "protect against pro-allergic sensitisation of TRAP [Traffic Related Air Pollution] exposure."41 So many benefits...

7. Ginger

This root herb is packed with benefits, and no doubt you have heard of it. A common culinary fixture, ginger is about more than flavor, but known to treat nausea, reduce muscle soreness, provide anti-inflammatory benefits, treat indigestion, help menstrual discomfort and battle infections. Regarding diabetes, ginger has been found to primarily do two things, reduce blood sugar levels and regulate insulin production, not to mention it has some potent anti-inflammatory42 properties that address the negative influence of air pollution and type 2 diabetes. This was concluded in a study performed in 2013 on the "Anti-inflammatory effects of zingiber officinale in type 2 diabetic patients." In fact, in scientific studies43 it has been "suggested that ginger, via it's major component, gingerol, by inhibition of key enzymes relevant to type 2 diabetes, α-glucosidase and α-amylase, are known to improve diabetes."44 Beyond this, it has even been linked to preventing various forms of cancer through the presence of gingerols, shogaol and paradols inherent to this precious root herb. This makes ginger pretty much a superstar when it comes to transforming your health, and as such, that makes it a major part of the protocol.

8. Magnesium

Toted as being of "chief physiological importance to the body"45, magnesium is one of those minerals which can be easy to overlook but which is so crucial to a properly functioning body, supporting so many processes, as well as being of vital importance to a person with diabetes. Magnesium reduces high blood pressure, helps protect the heart, relaxes muscles (stopping spasms,) improves digestion and promotes strong bone density. The correlation between diabetics and Magnesium is clear: diabetics are typically low and deficient in Magnesium and increasing it, "[improves] insulin sensitivity and metabolic control."46 Why does this matter? One of the benefits of Magnesium lies in it's ability to regulate blood sugar levels. Just taking 100mg a day, the "risk of diabetes is decreased by 15 percent in prediabetics and in those already with type 2 diabetes." Pretty major. The website for the American Diabetes Association published a study, where it was found that magnesium intake, "is significantly inversely associated with risk of type 2 diabetes."47

WHERE IT ALL BEGINS

So now you know the heart of the protocol: the Diabetes Reversing 8. Now what's left is knowing where to look for these precious substances, because the really good news is they are not nearly as exotic as they sound and are found in foods at your local grocery store for mere cents. In fact, they're probably already in your kitchen.

In the following tables, you will see where you can find the Diabetes Reversing 8, as well as the amounts of each super nutrient in each item. It will show to you that you don't need to be Greek, and living on a remote island, to live like the people of Halki!

THE DIABETES REVERSING 8 TABLE		
Super Nutrient	Food	Herbs/Spices
1. Glucoraphanin	Arugula Bok Choy Broccoli Broccoli Sprouts Brussel Sprouts Cabbage Cauliflower Collard Greens Kale Mustard Radish Turnip Watercress	
2. Sulforaphane	Arugula Bok Choy Broccoli Broccoli Sprouts Brussel Sprouts Cabbage Cauliflower Collard Greens Kale Mustard Radish Turnip Watercress	

THE DIABETES REVERSING 8 TABLE

Super Nutrient	Food	Herbs/Spices
3. Vitamin C	European Blackcurrants 202.7mg per cup Chilli (green) 109.1mg per pepper Orange Juice 124mg per cup Lemons 112.4mg per cup Cooked Kale 102mg per cup Broccoli 81mg per cup Cooked Tomatoes 55mg per cup Snow Peas 38mg Bell Peppers 190mg per cup Rose hip 541mg Kale 80mg per cup Garlic 31.2mg per cup Spinach 28mg	Dried Coriander Leaf 567mg Fresh Thyme 160mg Dried Parsley 122mg Fresh Dill Weed 85mg Ground cloves 81mg Saffron 81mg Pepper (Red or Cayenne) 76mg Paprika 71mg Chilli 64mg
4. Vitamin E	Almonds 7.3mg per 1 oz Almond Oil 5.3mg per tablespoon Avocado 4.2mg per avocado Brazil Nuts 1.6mg per 1 oz Broccoli 2.3 mg per cup Hazelnuts 4.3mg per 1 oz Hazelnut Oil 6.4mg per tablespoon Rice Bran Oil 4.4mg per tablespoon Pine Nuts 2.7mg per serving Spinach 3.7mg per cup Trout 2mg per fillet Salmon 2.0mg per fillet Red Bell Pepper 1.9mg Asparagus 1.5mg per 4 oz Spinach 2mg per 4 oz Dry Roasted Peanuts 1.4mg per 1 oz Sunflower Seeds 7.4mg per 1 oz Olive Oil 1.9mg per tablespoon Grapeseed Oil 3.9mg per tablespoon Wheatgerm Oil 149.4mg	Paprika 30mg Pepper (Red or Cayenne) 30mg Chilli Powder 29mg Curry Powder 22mg Dried Oregano 19mg Ground Ginger 18mg
5. β-Carotene	Lettuce 2456µg per cup Red Bell Pepper 2059µg per cup (cooked) Red Bell Pepper 1932µg per cup (raw) Mustard Greens 10360µg per cup Butternut Squash 9369µg per cup Cooked Carrots 12998µg per cup Cooked Beet Greens 6609µg per cup Cooked Dandelion Green 4137µg per cup Romain Lettuce 2456µg per cup Canned Pumpkin 17003µg per cup Peas 1216µg per cup Cooked Spinach 11318µg per cup Mashed Sweet Potatoes 13308µg per cup Cooked Kale 10624.9µg per cup Broccoli 1449µg per cup (cooked)	Fresh Basil 27323 mcg Paprika 19158 mcg Pepper (Red or Cayenne) 13735 mcg Chilli 9554mcg Fresh Thyme 5645 mcg Dried Basil 4449 mcg Dried Parsley 3899 mcg Dried Marjoram 3548 mcg Dried Oregano 2688 mcg Dried Coriander Leaf 2442 mcg

THE DIABETES REVERSING 8 TABLE		
Super Nutrient	**Food**	**Herbs/Spices**
6. Omega 3 fatty acid	Cod Liver Oil 2664mg per tablespoon Flaxseed Oil 12059mg per cup Flaxseeds 2338mg per tablespoon Walnut Oil 2353mg per cup Wheat Germ Oil 1561mg per cup Olive Oil 1644mg per cup Yogurt (Whole, Plain) 66.2mg per cup Salmon Oil 5038mg 1 tbsp Brussel Sprouts 270mg per cup Chia Seeds 5064mg per oz Flax Seeds 6479mg per oz Hemp Seeds 2641mg per oz Canned Sardines 1649mg per cup Mackerel 4107mg per serving Walnuts 2579mg per oz Atlantic Salmon 4252mg per 6 oz fillet	Fresh Basil 2747mg Dried Oregano 2732mg Ground Cloves 2649mg Dried Marjoram 2384mg Dried Tarragon 2004mg Dried Spearmint 1959mg Canned Capers 1600mg Fresh Spearmint 1536mg Yellow Mustard 1457mg Fresh Peppermint 1243mg
7. Ginger		
8. Magnesium	Almonds 77mg per 1 oz handful Artichokes 76.8mg per artichoke Avocado 58mg per avocado Brown Rice 85.8mg in 1 cup Black Turtle Beans 120.4mg in 1 cup White beans (navy) 96.4mg in 1 cup Cashews 82.9mg in 1 oz Cooked Swiss Chard 150.5mg Dark Chocolate 65mg per 1 oz Edamame 147.9mg in 1 cup Molasses 48.4mg per 1 tbsp Lima Beans 125.8mg in 1 cup Peanut Butter 57.3mg in 2 tbsp Pumpkin Seeds 156mg in 1 oz Cooked Quinoa 118.4mg in 1 cup Cooked Spinach 157mg in 1 cup Hemp Seeds 198.8mg in 1 oz Sunflower Seeds 91mg in 1 oz Yogurt (Whole, Plain) 29.4mg per cup Walnuts 126mg in 1 cup	Fresh Basil 556mg Dried Coriander Leaf 498mg Dried Spearmint 422mg Dried Dill Weed 357mg Dried Basil 336mg Fresh Thyme 317mg Canned Capers 287mg Fresh Spearmint 286mg Ground Sage 272mg Fresh Dill Weed 256mg Dried Marjoram 255mg Dried Tarragon 235mg Fresh Peppermint 229mg Celery Seed 225mg Fennel Seed 223mg Coriander Seed 221mg Table Salt 200mg

SPICING THINGS UP

You'll see in the table above, various herbs and spices and how they can be categorized according to the Diabetes Reversing 8. It isn't only food that offers diabetes-reversing effects, herbs and spices are powerhouse sources of these nutrients too and are a great asset on the protocol. They are also true to the people of Halki and their lifestyle, being a staple of the Mediterranean diet and, most importantly, Alexander Doukis' notes. In Northern America we tend to overlook a good majority of spices and stick to just a couple at best. Yet herbs have much more to offer beside flavor, they possess so many more amazing gifts, gifts that will aid your Halki Remedy protocol.

From a practical, taste-promoting angle, herbs and spices will take your dips and dressings up another level, and they will be an easy way to boost the diabetes reversing power of your culinary creations. It's a no lose situation.

This may be news to you if you only viewed herbs and spices as providing taste benefits. But historically they have been used to support the entire body and provide essential nutrients, as a kind of medicine. Make sure you have lots of herbs, in both dried and fresh forms, and use them often.

THE MAGIC OF BROCCOLI

You'll notice that broccoli features in a lot of the recipes in this plan, and this is for good reason. This is because of science; your mom wasn't wrong when she told you to eat your broccoli, but only now are we understanding why it's so good for us. Cruciferous vegetables are a great source of fiber, vitamins and disease-preventing/reversing phytochemicals. Pretty much everything you would want from food. The disease preventing/reversing part wasn't an exaggeration either. The National Cancer Institute has researched cruciferous vegetables extensively for their disease- fighting capacities, and have concluded, that the compounds found in cruciferous vegetables fight disease in the following ways:

- They help protect cells from DNA damage.

- They help inactivate carcinogens.

- They have antiviral and antibacterial effects.

- They have anti-inflammatory effects.
- They induce cell death (apoptosis).
- They inhibit tumor blood vessel formation (angiogenesis) and tumor cell migration (needed for metastasis).

Two of the reasons why cruciferous vegetables are so valuable have already been introduced above—glucophanin and sulforaphane—which offer protective effects against toxins49 and are chemopreventive.

While the people of Halki ate broccoli sprouts for their disease-reversing power, in our protocol we'll employ the wholesome goodness of other cruciferous vegetables to generate the same effect.

NOT YOUR AVERAGE DIABETES HEALTH PLAN

Unlike so many other health plans for diabetes, or advice from your doctor—to start with weight loss, exercise and "healthy eating"—the Halki Diabetes Remedy will not give you that frustratingly vague, generic advice. Such advice merely adds to a person's confusion, discouragement and feeling of being overwhelmed, since it is never that simple. Sure, it sounds like a simple instruction, but not when there are conflicting views on what constitutes 'healthy.' Even professionals acknowledge that "...there are multiple nutrition guidelines (some of which are unclear or conflicting) [and that]... clinicians often find patients confused about their nutrition

therapy and ultimately about what foods to eat."51 This can be especially confusing when

recommended to people who already considered themselves to have a healthy lifestyle, but have developed type 2 diabetes anyway.

As already shown, this eBook won't promote generic advice, but specific facts and plans to bring about a positive change in your condition. It won't tell you to 'eat healthy' and just munch on celery, because that won't work. The real power lies in adopting the right substances into your preexisting lifestyle. And that's what the protocol does.

UNDERSTANDING THE PROTOCOL

The great thing about this protocol is you don't have to know why something works, in order for it to work. However, knowing why certain things are important and how they will help the process you will be undertaking, can be useful. The following bullet points highlight some of the 'whys,' to help you understand what you will get from following the protocol exactly.

• Don't skimp on the oil. If you come from a typical dieting background and have developed the mindset that fat and oils are bad, you will probably be tempted to skip or cut back on the oil. DO NOT DO THIS. Hopefully, by now you've accepted the fact that fats are not uniformly unhealthy for us and aren't the reason for type

2 diabetes. Wisely chosen, they make you healthy! Not only are they a staple of the mediterranean diet, but research is proving how the right oils actually improve how your body deals with food, making nutrients and protective phytochemicals more bioavailable. Wendy White, an associate professor of food science and human nutrition, conducted an experiment in 2017 and concluded, "...the amount of oil added to the vegetables had a proportional relationship with the amount of nutrient absorption."52 Simply explained: more oil, means more absorption. Whilst I wouldn't suggest drinking oil like you would water, it's also not something to be afraid of, especially when it helps your body utilize what you eat. And this isn't the only benefit of using oil on your veggies, oils will be one of the main sources of Omega 3 fatty acids on the protocol. This is the substance needed to combat inflammation; making oils a crucial component in the dressings, dips and sauces. And before you think of getting the low-fat version of salad dressings, they won't get the nutrients out of your food.53 There is definitely no need to be scared of the right kind of fats, they will be one of your greatest allies on this protocol. There are some oils which are very high in their Omega 3 content, such as wheatgerm or walnut, but you may not find these on the shelves of your local Walmart. Because of this, the recipes in the protocol focus on canola oil, an oil which is supremely high in Omega 3 content, whilst also being widely available at regular grocery stores. However, if you can get your hands on other oils, or feel like ordering them online, don't feel restricted in any way. Check "The Diabetes Reversing 8 Table" for their Omega 3 content and use them as you wish. If they are higher than the Omega content found in canola oil, even better! In a similar way, avocado is often used in the protocol recipes, not only as a source of vitamin e, but since research has proven it's ability to optimize nutrient absorption, specifically the absorption of beta-carotene. In the past, people may have shied away from eating such a food because of the fat, but now we know it is that very factor which makes such foods amazing for us and our health.

• The role of magnesium There is increasingly more interest in magnesium as scientists discover the critical role it plays in the perpetuation and worsening of diabetes. It has actually

been identified as an "essential mineral in the regulation of blood sugar, playing a part in the secretion and function of insulin by opening cell membranes for glucose. Low blood levels of magnesium are frequently seen in people with type 2 diabetes. A deficiency can cause insulin resistance, so that they require greater amounts of insulin to maintain their blood sugar within normal levels."54 This would certainly warrant dietary inclusion of this mineral. Check the Diabetes Reversing 8 table and look at the foods which are high in Magnesium. Include these in your diet, add appropriate items to your dips and incorporate them into your lifestyle for sustained health. You can look into getting magnesium supplements, however, these are not necessary when you are getting this mineral through your food. Scientists confirm that dietary sources of vitamins and minerals always trump capsules and tablets (although capsules and tablets can have their place in a well-rounded diet) and that is why these dressings and dips are such a great vehicle for minerals like magnesium.

• Emphasis on getting vitamins from food. It can be easy to think getting vitamins through supplements are the answer. Our human mind quite likes the idea of the apparent "quick fix"

of that approach, however the Halki Diabetes Remedy is based on long-standing research, and when it comes to vitamins, as explained by Dr. Clifford Lo, an associate professor of nutrition at the Harvard School of Public Health, "nutrients are most potent when they come from food. They are accompanied by many nonessential but beneficial nutrients, such as hundreds of carotenoids, flavonoids, minerals, and antioxidants that aren't in most supplements."55 When you eat a certain food, you get the whole vitamin 'package,' exactly the way nature designed the vitamin to be transported into your system. There are times when supplements will be suggested on this plan, but they have been incorporated into the protocol purposefully. That's the great thing about the protocol, everything you need is in the dips and dressings, and the daily pairings—you won't need to get vitamins from supplements—but the supplements which are suggested in this eBook just give you an above and beyond advantage.

• Bioaccessibility is the process by which macro and micronutrients from food are processed by the body in order to be utilized. This is what we want to maximize on the protocol, through certain food pairings and pureeing techniques. While macronutrients are fairly easy for the

body to process, micronutrients are a little trickier and require specific conditions for this to happen. The Halki Diabetes Remedy takes this into account so you don't miss what you really need.

• Drinking your food. Cooking or liquifying food makes it more bioavailable. The natural consequence of pureeing food is that the nutrients become easier to absorb. That's the beauty of packing the dips, dressings and sauces with all the nutrients possible and taking it in it's

liquified form. If you're having a thicker dip, all that needs to be done is extra chewing, which will do the same thing to break down the food and make it bioavailable.

• Watch how you prep that broccoli. Just by preparing a food in a certain way, you can unlock the full potential of the food. Sulforaphane, one of the main reasons broccoli is so

amazing, has to be prepared in a specific way to get the full benefit. We've already discussed how cooking foods can make certain nutrients bioavailable. This is also true for broccoli. By steaming the broccoli before use you will maximize the sulforaphane content.

Then, pairing the broccoli with a myrosinase-rich item, such as arugula, wasabi or mustard seed, further unlocks this potential. Consideration of these details can take the protocol to the next level.

• The 'how' matters - food pairing matters, liquifying it matters, understanding how to unlock the power of the micronutrients in the food you're prepping matters. Steaming vegetables will be the preferred method of cooking, if you want to fully utilize that vegetable's power. If you're a fan of microwaving, I hate to burst your convenience bubble, but this will destroy the majority of enzymes and other beneficial substances within the broccoli that you really want to keep. Blasting a food with microwaves, stops any chance of those benefits. Elizabeth Jeffery, PhD, a researcher at the University of Illinois, states that we need to cook our food with more than just flavor or microbiological safety in mind: "Now our task is to go further. Processing can ensure that the bioactives – the cancer protective compounds – arrive in your digestive system in a form the body can use."56 There are certain foods where the 'how' is just as important as the 'what,' in other words, how you prepare the tomatoes or broccoli etc is as important as eating the food in the first place. It's good to know you'll be getting the most from your food, and these simple considerations and adjustments will enable this.

HOW IT ALL WORKS

PAIRING UP

As mentioned, this is a very specifically designed protocol. The Diabetes Reversing 8 are tracked in each individual dip and dressing and then paired with another for that day, so they can work synergistically to give you what you need. Nothing in this protocol is random, every item has been consciously selected to work together. One of the interesting outcomes of modern-day scientific research is the finding that, "Pairing certain foods together is more than just about taste

- specific foods eaten together can help your body utilize the benefits more effectively."

In the protocol there are a variety of recipes, so you don't get bored of certain combinations or flavors. You should not break up the daily pairings, although you can switch them around within that day. One of the reasons each recipe shows a table underneath is so you can start to correlate the food you are eating with how it ticks the boxes of each of the Diabetes Reversing 8 items. You will start to notice that when ginger, for example, is absent from a recipe, you need to ensure you get ginger in another form, such as ginger tea or a supplement. This will help you become a part of the process and start to understand the deeper elements of what you are eating.

SUPPLEMENTATION

While the goal is to get as many of the Diabetes Reversing 8 from food, there will be times when supplementation is warranted and has been added to the protocol. You will see this announced at the top of each new day in a small table. However, like the rest of this protocol, complexity is never the goal. You won't be required to take a thousand capsules a day. The only time you will be required to take additional support through supplements are with meals that don't feature some kind of cruciferous vegetable or ginger. Because these nutrients are so crucial, if a meal doesn't feature them it is still necessary to get them in some form, and this is when supplements are advised.

Thankfully, because of the wonders of the internet, these supplements are never far away. At the touch of a button you can have a quality product in your virtual grocery basket and shortly after dispatched to your home. If you like to shop the old-fashioned way, there are still ways to get these supplements, since they are not rare by any means. Whatever way works for you is perfect, so long as you make sure you have access to these supplements on the required days.

The two supplements you will need are:

1)   A sulforaphane supplement which features myrosinase (so the glucosinolates are converted into sulforaphane.)

2)   A ginger root supplement, so you can get at least another 1000mg a day.

GINGER TEA

There is another way to make sure you get your daily dose of ginger, and since there are just some dips and dressings that don't lend themselves to this particular flavor, there will be times when ginger tea may be an easier way to boost your intake of this beneficial herb.

And fortunately, it's pretty darn tasty.

Ginger tea is simple to make and boasts a range of health benefits. It doesn't matter if you decide to use the fresh root form or use powdered. I personally like to use both versions— powdered and fresh—depending on what I have to hand.

To make ginger tea:

1.   Place 1 ½ tsp freshly grated or sliced ginger root (or powder equivalent) into a mug.

2.   Fill the mug with boiling water, to the top.

3.   Leave for 10 minutes, for the ginger to infuse.

4.   After the 10 minutes has passed, strain the ginger tea so there is no residue of the ginger root and you are just left with the liquid.

5.   Honey or lemon can be added. If you prefer a low-glycemic option, stevia powder or liquid can be used.

SERVING SUGGESTIONS

The serving suggestions are definitely not limited to what has been recommended beneath the recipe, you can choose to have anything you want with a dip or dressing, beyond what has been suggested. That's the beauty of this protocol—it works around your preexisting lifestyle. If you notice the glucophanin/sulforaphane boxes are unchecked, feel free to add any cruciferous vegetables you feel like or have left over from the week (you really can't go wrong with cruciferous vegetables!) However, if these boxes are unchecked, the serving suggestion for that day will also act as a reminder, so you don't have to worry about missing anything.

The serving suggestions have been added for their nutritional value, but beyond this you can add bread, chips, rice, pasta, pizza, fries.... anything you choose which is part of your regular diet.

THE MULTITASKERS OF THE GROUP

There are certain items in the Diabetes Reversing 8 table that provide multiple benefits and are therefore an easy way to see that all your bases are covered in the easiest way possible. Below are a few of the items that will allow you to easily take a dressing or dip up a notch. Add them where you can, even if it isn't necessarily mentioned in the recipe.

Basil - If you've studied the Diabetes Reversing 8 table, you'll notice this herb is present—and in 1st place—in 3 of the 8 super nutrient categories. Eat fresh basil, and you'll be covering multiple bases and reaping the benefits. Basil is loaded with Magnesium, Omega 3 and β-Carotene, it is an incredible source of anti-oxidants, two of which, orientin and viceninare, protect white blood cells which support immune function. For the sake of the recipes in this book, fresh basil is preferred over dried since it will provide the maximum amount of valuable oils in the basil leaves. Lemons - Not only is it called for in dressings as a great source of vitamin c, but this citrus fruit can do amazing things when squeezed on steamed broccoli, bringing the mellow, earthy taste of broccoli a lifted, citrus twist. If you're not such a fan of broccoli, this can make a big difference.

Chili - This means chili in all it's forms: fresh, dried, paprika, red pepper, fresh green chili, chili flakes etc. Similar to basil, these spices are present on 3 of the 8 super nutrients and offer a wide range of benefits. If you can stand the heat, add as much as you can—exceed the amount given in the recipes—and your health will thank you!

Broccoli - In this eBook I've included a fair number of dip recipes featuring broccoli, but this isn't typically a number one ingredient where dips are concerned (which is a real shame, considering how good it is for us.) So even though a dip may not feature this amazing ingredient, don't feel like you can't eat it on the side. In fact, I would encourage this! It is frequently mentioned in the serving suggestions, and even when it isn't, don't let this stop you from having some anyway! Chew it well, add something spicy if possible (mustard, horseradish, wasabi etc) if the accompanying dip doesn't feature such an ingredient, and enjoy the health benefits.

IF YOU READ NOTHING ELSE, READ THIS

We've all been guilty of speed-reading a book, skipping huge sections and jumping to the most relevant parts. In our busy lives we just don't have the time to do everything and I know there will be a lot of people that struggle to read through this entire eBook. It is my hope that everyone can read this book from start to finish, but that's not always reality. This section will help those who don't have time for all the history and science but just want to get down to business. In this section you'll find an amalgamation of the protocol's basic guidelines as well as frequently asked questions. I would still encourage you to go back and read from the beginning, but if that isn't possible, this chapter contains a lot of what you need to know. And even if you have read the entire eBook thus far—big thumbs up from me—you'll benefit from this chapter too.

I can't eat certain foods featured in the recipes. What should I do?

If you have allergies to any of the recipe ingredients, that is a good reason to leave them out! If a recipe suggests nuts or other items which you cannot eat, look at "The Diabetes Reversing 8 Table" on pages 32-34 and see if there is a logical substitution within the same category. Locate the ingredient you want to remove, note the super nutrient category it is within and look for an suitable replacement within that same category. For example, in the case of nuts (which are in the magnesium category) using avocado, white beans, lima beans, pumpkin seeds or hemp seeds would be good alternatives.

The alternative may or may not offer the same taste or amount of that super nutrient, but will help complete the dip/dressing and fulfil that super nutrient category.

Can I change ingredients?

The protocol has been developed purposefully but this does not mean it's inflexible. There is a certain amount of leeway in each of the recipes and the day-to-day pairings themselves. Whilst you cannot completely dissemble the protocol, you can tailor parts of it. You can change ingredients, but the more you change the original recipe the more "mental rearranging" is required from you. Often, unless you are deathly allergic to a food, it may just be easier to leave it in the recipe and "buffer" it's taste by adding in other ingredients which you DO like (see question below) or combine it with a meal you really enjoy.

Can I add other ingredients to the recipes?

As mentioned above, this is an option. The recipes in the protocol have deliberately been kept very basic. There aren't 100 ingredients. In fact, the maximum number of ingredients in a recipe is 6. This isn't a gourmet cookbook—it's a health plan which is meant for as many people as possible and complexity defeats the purpose of this protocol. The basic recipes provided can be a great foundation for any other ingredients you feel would round out the recipe to your particular tase. Adding to a recipe is easier than taking ingredients away and doesn't require any additional "calculating."

Do I have to follow the serving suggestions?

At the end of certain recipes there will be an additional sentence or two labelled "serving suggestions." These may not be part of the recipes themselves but they are still an important part of the protocol and should not be overlooked. The main purpose for these suggestions is to complete and complement the ingredients in the dressing. Most of the time these suggestions will recommend cruciferous vegetables. Cruciferous vegetables are a key component to fulfilling the Diabetes Reversing 8, because of their sulforaphane content, but they are not listed in the recipes because most people don't eat broccoli or red cabbage dressing—though this doesn't have to stop you from liquidizing these vegetables if you feel adventurous! To remedy this they are included as a serving suggestion or as a supplement.

Do I need certain pieces of equipment to make this protocol work?

There are major benefits to blending food (as has been discussed in earlier sections of this book.) However, if you do not have or cannot afford a blender or food processor it is not impossible to do this protocol. Whilst it is ideal to blend the recipes—so phytonutrients and other precious components within the foods become more bioavailable—the recipes can often be finely chopped, minced and then shaken in a jar. (This is a good back-up method even for those who do have a blender or food processor.) If money is an issue you can get good used kitchen equipment online. Even if all you have is an old-style glass blender, that will do. Start anywhere with the protocol, invest as much money as you can, but don't let these limitations stop you from beginning somewhere. You don't need expensive equipment to succeed with this plan. Fancy blenders, food processors etc are great, but if all you have is a glass jar or a second-hand blender these can do the job just fine.

I just looked at the protocol. What does the layout mean?

The 21 Day Plan is presented so you can understand exactly what is required on each day. Not only will you find the recipes and their instructions, you will find a small table showing what supplements are required for that day (at the top of each day) as well as a larger table breaking down each of the Diabetes Reversing 8 (beneath each recipe.) The supplemental table should be self explanatory, it will tell you whether a ginger or sulforaphane supplement is needed that day, based on the recipes. The table below each recipe highlights which of the Diabetes Reversing 8 is present within that recipe. Some may not have certain boxes ticked, not all of them will, but don't worry, because the serving suggestions, the supplemental suggestion and the following recipe for that day will take this into account. This is a well calculated plan and you will be informed of exactly what you need every step of the way. Make sure you check, and are familiar with, the 21 Day Plan so you can see exactly how these dips, dressings, and sauces are paired on a day-to-day basis. They have been paired for a reason and balance out the day so you're never in deficit of what you need.

There are some dressings I don't think I will like. Can I leave these out?

You can, but there are a few guidelines which need to be followed.

1) It's important to keep the recipe pairings together. This would mean thinking of the two recipes on each day as a kind of unit. You can't suddenly pair recipe no. 2 from day 8 with recipe no. 1 from day 21.) This would be fragmenting the units. If you only like one recipe in a certain day you can't just have that recipe, you'll need to replace them both.

2) Make sure you adhere to the supplement table (the table at the beginning of each day) and any serving suggestions for that particular day. If you replace one set of dressings for another you need to replace everything else with it too—supplement table, serving suggestions, everything... Move that entire day.

3) Consider how removing certain days and replacing them with others in the protocol will impact the foods you need to buy each week. Additional planning is required when you replace certain days. Make sure you don't get confused and you know exactly what you're eating and when.

Can I do more than just make dressings?

The protocol is composed of the dressings, the serving suggestions and supplements. However, you can fill your diet with as many of the foods listed in "The Diabetes Reversing 8 Table"—on pages 32-34—as you choose. I'm a big proponent of slow and steady; I often feel it's unwise to change too much, too fast. You certainly don't need to overhaul your entire lifestyle but you certainly won't do any harm by incorporating more of the Diabetes Reversing 8 into it. You can't over-do the good stuff. Just know that the protocol itself will be enough to make changes.

Why do I need to look at "The Diabetes Reversing 8 Table" and what is it?

This table might initially be overlooked, yet it is very important. The beauty of the 21 Day Plan is that you don't have to think much, the thinking has been done for you, you just need to follow. However, "The Diabetes Reversing 8 Table" allows you to tailor things to your needs, it will give examples of how you can obtain super nutrients from everyday items and tell you how much of that super nutrient is present with the food. Whilst it is important to keep the dressings in their daily pairings, the ingredients are not absolutely set in stone. As already explained, there will be times when an ingredient isn't appropriate for you or isn't readily available where you live. Don't despair, you won't miss out! Refer back to "The Diabetes Reversing 8 Table" (pages 32-34) to get guidance on a good substitute. Whatever ingredient needs to be omitted from the recipe can be replaced with another from the same group. Also take a look at the number beside the ingredient. This will inform you of how much of that super nutrient is present within that food. Go for the highest measurement possible.

If I'm taking the supplements (ginger and sulforaphane) how much do I need to take?

The recommended daily dosage for treating diabetes is: 1600mg ginger and 40-60mg sulforaphane.

Can I take daily sulforaphane supplements, as well as the dressings or any other cruciferous vegetables?

There is no harm in combining different sources of sulforaphane and taking sulforaphane supplements daily as well as cruciferous vegetables. This will be very effective. If you have access to supplements then it is a good idea to use them—although it is not the only option, so you don't need to worry if you cannot buy them (more about this in the question below.) Thankfully, because of the internet, it is a lot easier these days to purchase more specialized items such as sulforaphane supplements. There isn't really a limit on how much sulforaphane you can safely consume, and it's hard to consume a detrimental amount of sulforaphane from food. You would have to eat a lot. So feel free to incorporate as much sulforaphane into your day as you can.

What if I can't get supplements where I live?

Don't despair if you can't buy supplements. You will see that supplements—ginger and sulforaphane—are suggested for this plan at the top of each day. If you cannot obtain these supplements there is an alternative, though it may not be as simple as swallowing a pill. If you cannot buy ginger supplements look at making ginger tea from the fresh root (the recipe for this is found on page 40) and include extra ginger in the recipes, even if the recipe doesn't list it. Taste

wise, this may not be the best, but determine how you are willing to compensate for the absence of supplementation and include this in the protocol.

Sulforaphane can also be obtained through food. If you cannot get supplements, pay extra attention to sulforaphane-rich foods (e.g. broccoli) and consume these alongside your meals. When eating broccoli—or any cruciferous vegetable—you need to pair it with items such as horseradish or mustard in order to "unlock" the sulforaphane. Cruciferous vegetables are still good on their own, but you will not be getting the most from them unless they are combined with a food such as mustard or horseradish.

How long do I need to do the protocol? Will I need to be on it for the rest of my life? Everyone is different and your journey will be unique to you. There is no set timeline but you certainly should not need to be on it for the rest of your life. Put all your energy into living the

protocol as best as you can and let your body do what it is going to do. Like every good journey, it takes faith to take that first step and requires frequent assessment to work out where you are and how you will get closer to your end goal. Assess as you go.

Something on the protocol goes against my doctor's advise. What should I do?

Build the protocol around your doctor-approved recommendations. The 21 Day Plan is a supplemental plan, it does not replace what you normally eat or what you are currently doing (which may be governed by your doctor.) If you have been advised to eat a certain way by your healthcare provider, do not abandon this, or feel you have to in order to experience The Halki Diabetes Remedy. The dressings and dips within this eBook are meant to be an addition to the way you eat, not to override it or act as a replacement. If an ingredient in any of the recipes contradict what you are currently eating, and have been advised to eat, see how you can potentially replace the ingredient— consult "The Diabetes Reversing 8 Table" on pages 32-34—and select a logical substitution (based on the instruction provided above.) This eBook does not advise that you drop your medication or eat anything which is in direct opposition with your medication requirements or Doctor's advise. Use discernment.

How much dressing do I need to eat? Can I eat more/less than the recipe states?

You don't need to eat a large amount of a dressing or dip to experience the benefits. Each recipe in the protocol typically caters for 1-2 people, however, since an ideal portion size can vary from person to person, you can tailor the recipe amount to suit your needs. If you find you have more than you need, store the remaining dressing in the fridge, or freeze it for later. You cannot over- do these dressings! If you want a bigger serving, make more and help yourself! On the other hand, if you don't have a large appetite, you don't have to force the entire dressing down. The quantity of the dressing makes no difference, you don't have to consume a bucket-load of dressing to experience the benefits, what makes the difference is having the Diabetes Reversing 8 in your day. Make the recipes work for you.

How much is an adequate serving of cruciferous vegetables? Do I have to eat a lot?

Of course, it's good if you can eat as many cruciferous vegetables as possible, but who among us wants to be eating broccoli for breakfast, lunch and dinner? You shouldn't have to overwhelm your diet with these vegetables, but you do need a healthy amount in your day. A couple of cups would be a healthy, sustaining serving.

I don't live in the US and don't use the measurements listed in the recipes... how can I convert them?

There is information online about converting different measurement systems, however, to help you out, we've included a conversion table below.

MEASUREMENT CONVERSION CHART	
SPOONS & CUPS	ML
1/8 tsp	0.5 ml
1/4 tsp	1 ml
1/2 tsp	2.5 ml
1 tsp	5 ml
1 tbsp	15 ml
2 tbsp	30 ml
1/4 cup	60 ml
1/3 cup	80 ml
1/2 cup	125 ml
2/3 cup	165 ml
3/4 cup	190 ml
1 cup	250 ml

RECIPES

Welcome to the recipe section, where you will see how the scientific research about the Diabetes Reversing 8 translates to the kitchen and how you live your daily life. As you read through these recipes it should become clear how easy it is to get these precious substances through your food. If we could live on broccoli sprouts and other exotic items in our regular American lives, that would be great, however I don't often see those things in the aisles of my local grocery store. These recipes will show that you don't need those exotic items to experience the benefits of the Halki Diabetes Remedy, you can get them wherever you normally shop.

If you looked at the Diabetes Reversing 8 table and noticed certain foods which you adore, fabulous! Feel free to consciously include them in your daily meals, and now you know that your favorite food is also doing you good! Snack on those items as much as you want. You may even discover a few new favorites by venturing out and trying something new. Surrounding yourself with these health-enhancing, diabetes-reversing foods, in addition to the set daily dips and dressings, will be a total game changer. You can't go wrong

Week 1

Supplements	Needed Today?
GINGER	YES
SULFORAPHANE	NO

Avocado Horseradish Spread

Total time: 5 minutes

1 avocado

1 tbsp onion, finely chopped 1 tbsp lemon juice

1 tbsp horseradish, grated

1.Mix together all the ingredients in a food processor or blender until well combined.

Serving suggestion: Make the most of the horseradish, and it's sulforaphane-enhancing properties, by adding cruciferous vegetables—preferably broccoli or cauliflower—to this meal.

Gluco-raphanin	Sulfora-phane	Vitamin C	Vitamin E	β-Carotene	Omega 3	Ginger	Magnesium
X	X	X	X				X

Oregano Dressing

Total time: 5 minutes

2 tbsp lemon juice

4 tbsp oil (refer to the table on page 34 for oil suggestions)

½ tsp dried oregano

¼ garlic clove Pinch black pepper

1.   Combine all the ingredients in a food processor or blender and blend until smooth. If using a food processor, add the oil slowly as the food processor runs.

Serving suggestion: 1 tsp of fresh ginger can be added to this dressing. It will alter the taste. But if you don't have access to supplements, if you don't want to drink ginger tea, or if you just want to bump up your ginger quota for the day, this can be an option.

*   If you can, take sulforaphane supplements, even if there are cruciferous vegetables in the recipe or serving suggestion.

Gluco-raphanin	Sulfora-phane	Vitamin C	Vitamin E	β-Carotene	Omega 3	Ginger	Magnesium
		X	X	X	X		

Day 2

Supplements	Needed Today?
GINGER	NO
SULFORAPHANE	YES

Tomato Vinaigrette

Total Time: 5 minutes

1 tbsp apple cider vinegar

½ clove of garlic

½ tsp mustard

1 tbsp fresh basil, minced 5 grape tomatoes

2 tbsp oil (refer to the table on page 34 for oil suggestions)

1.   Combine all the ingredients in a food processor or blender and blend until smooth. If using a food processor, add the oil slowly as the food processor runs.

Serving suggestion: Serve this vinaigrette with steamed broccoli, cauliflower or any other cruciferous vegetables.

Gluco-raphanin	Sulfora-phane	Vitamin C	Vitamin E	β-Carotene	Omega 3	Ginger	Magnesium
		X	X	X	X		X

Lemon-Ginger Dressing

Total time: 10 minutes

3 tbsp oil (refer to the table on page 34 for oil suggestions)

2 tbsp lemon juice

1 tbsp apple cider vinegar 2 tsp fresh ginger, minced

1. Mix all the ingredients together in a bowl, a jar or a blender.

Serving suggestion: You should have had cruciferous vegetables earlier in the day— meaning no more is required—so this dressing can be matched with whatever food you choose.

* If you can, take sulforaphane supplements, even if there are cruciferous vegetables in the recipe or serving suggestion.

Gluco-raphanin	Sulfora-phane	Vitamin C	Vitamin E	β-Carotene	Omega 3	Ginger	Magnesium
		X			X	X	

Day 3

Supplements	Needed Today?
GINGER	NO
SULFORAPHANE	NO

Basil Ginger Dressing

Total time: 5 minutes

2 tbsp fresh basil, loosely packed 1 tbsp lemon juice

1 tsp fresh ginger, minced

¼ cup oil (refer to the table on page 34 for oil suggestions)

1. Process the basil, lemon juice and ginger in a food processor until smooth.

2. As the processor is running, slowly pour the oil into the mixture.

Serving suggestion: No set requirements for this dressing.

Gluco-raphanin	Sulfora-phane	Vitamin C	Vitamin E	β-Carotene	Omega 3	Ginger	Magnesium
		X		X	X	X	X

Almond Butter Dressing

Total time: 5 minutes

2 tbsp water

½ tsp mustard

2 tbsp almond butter

1 tbsp oil (refer to the table on page 34 for oil suggestions)

1 tbsp apple cider vinegar

1.   Combine all the ingredients in a food processor or blender and blend until smooth. If using a food processor, add the oil slowly as the food processor runs.

Serving suggestion: Make sure you have a serving of cruciferous vegetables—preferably broccoli or cauliflower. The sulforaphane content will be supported by the presence of mustard in this dressing.

*   If you can, take sulforaphane supplements, even if there are cruciferous vegetables in the recipe or serving suggestion.

Gluco-raphanin	Sulfora-phane	Vitamin C	Vitamin E	β-Carotene	Omega 3	Ginger	Magnesium
X	X		X		X		X

Day 4

Supplements	Needed Today?
GINGER	YES
SULFORAPHANE	NO

Greek Herb Dressing

Total time 5 minutes

¼ cup yogurt

1 tbsp olive/almond oil 1 tsp lemon juice

1 tsp fresh mint, chopped

1 tsp fresh dill weed, chopped

(Optional) Pinch of Himalayan salt and black peppe

1.   Combine all the ingredients in a food processor or blender and blend until smooth. If using a food processor, add the oil slowly as the food processor runs.

Serving suggestion: 1 tsp of fresh ginger can be added to this dressing. It will alter the taste. But if you don't have access to supplements, if you don't want to drink ginger tea, or if you just want to bump up your ginger quota for the day, this can be an option.

Gluco-raphanin	Sulfora-phane	Vitamin C	Vitamin E	β-Carotene	Omega 3	Ginger	Magnesium
		X	X		X		X

Arugula Basil Dip

Total time: 5 minutes

¼ cup arugula leaves, chopped 2 tbsp fresh basil

¼ cup almonds

3 tbsp lemon juice

1.   Place almonds in a bowl of water overnight to soak and soften. If you are short on time they can be submerged in boiling water for 3-4 minutes, or if you really don't have time, they can be thrown in a food processor as they are (but more oil may be needed if the almonds are dry and you won't be getting the full nutritional potential of the almonds if you don't soak them.)

2.   In a processor or blender, place the arugula, basil, almonds, and lemon juice, processing until completely smooth.

Serving suggestion: A dollop of mustard or horseradish will unlock the sulforaphane content in the arugula. You can add this to the dressing itself or leave it on the side.

*   If you can, take sulforaphane supplements, even if there are cruciferous vegetables in the recipe or serving suggestion.

Gluco-raphanin	Sulfora-phane	Vitamin C	Vitamin E	β-Carotene	Omega 3	Ginger	Magnesium
x	x	x	x	x	x		x

Day 5

Supplements	Needed Today?
GINGER	NO
SULFORAPHANE	YES

Ginger Mint Sauce

Total time: 10 minutes

3 tbsp plain yogurt

1 tsp fresh ginger, grated 3 tsp lemon juice

1 tsp oil (refer to the table on page 34 for oil suggestions)

2 tsp fresh mint, minced

1. Combine all the ingredients in a food processor or blender and blend until smooth. If using a food processor, add the oil slowly as the food processor runs.

Serving suggestion: Today you will need a side of cruciferous vegetables—preferably broccoli or cauliflower. Pair with a dollop of mustard/horseradish.

Gluco-raphanin	Sulfora-phane	Vitamin C	Vitamin E	β-Carotene	Omega 3	Ginger	Magnesium
		X			X	X	X

Herby Parmesan Nut Dip

Total time: 10 minutes

3 tbsp fresh basil

¼ cup almonds

⅓ cup finely grated parmesan cheese

3 tbsp oil (refer to the table on page 34 for oil suggestions)

1.   Place almonds in a bowl of water overnight to soak and soften. If you are short on time they can be submerged in boiling water for 3-4 minutes, or if you really don't have time, they can be thrown in a food processor as they are (but more oil may be needed if the almonds are dry and you won't be getting the full nutritional potential of the almonds if you don't soak them.)

2.   Place the basil leaves, almonds, parmesan (and oil, if using a blender) in a food processor or blender. Process until it reaches a fine consistency.

3.   If using a food processor, and not a high speed blender, gradually add the oil until well mixed.

Serving suggestion: No requirements for this dip. Can be paired with anything of your choosing.

*   If you can, take sulforaphane supplements, even if there are cruciferous vegetables in the recipe or serving suggestion.

Gluco-raphanin	Sulfora-phane	Vitamin C	Vitamin E	β-Carotene	Omega 3	Ginger	Magnesium
			X	X	X		X

Day 6

Supplements	Needed Today?
GINGER	YES
SULFORAPHANE	NO

Citrus Dressing

Total Time: 20 minutes

2 tbsp lemon juice

¼ cup arugula

½ avocado

2 tbsp oil (refer to the table on page 34 for oil suggestions)

1.   Combine all the ingredients in a food processor or blender and blend until smooth. If using a food processor, add the oil slowly as the food processor runs.

Serving suggestion: Serve with a dollop of mustard or horseradish and eat with anything else you wish.

Gluco-raphanin	Sulfora-phane	Vitamin C	Vitamin E	β-Carotene	Omega 3	Ginger	Magnesium
x	x	x	x		x		x

Black Bean Dip

Total Time: 10 minutes

6 tbsp tomatoes, seeded and diced 6 tbsp black beans

½ avocado

1 tsp lime juice 2 tbsp basil

1.   Chop the tomatoes, remove the seeds, and place the chopped tomatoes in a big bowl.

2.   Open the can of black beans, rinse and drain, and add to the bowl with the tomatoes.

3.   Next, add the avocado, lime juice, and basil to the same mixing bowl and mix well.

Serving suggestion: 1 tsp of fresh ginger can be added to this dressing. It will alter the taste. But if you don't have access to supplements, if you don't want to drink ginger tea, or if you just want to bump up your ginger quota for the day, this can be an option.

*   If you can, take sulforaphane supplements, even if there are cruciferous vegetables in the recipe or serving suggestion.

Gluco-raphanin	Sulfora-phane	Vitamin C	Vitamin E	β-Carotene	Omega 3	Ginger	Magnesium
		X	X	X	X		X

Day 7

Supplements	Needed Today?
GINGER	NO
SULFORAPHANE	YES

Lime Ginger Dressing

Total time: 5 minutes

3 tbsp plain yogurt 1 tbsp fresh cilantro 1 tbsp lime juice

1 tbsp oil (refer to the table on page 34 for oil suggestions)

½ tsp fresh ginger, minced

¼ clove garlic

1.   Combine all the ingredients in a food processor or blender and blend until smooth. If using a food processor, add the oil slowly as the food processor runs.

Serving suggestion: No requirements with this dressing. Best to take sulforaphane supplements today if you can.

Gluco-raphanin	Sulfora-phane	Vitamin C	Vitamin E	β-Carotene	Omega 3	Ginger	Magnesium
		X			X	X	X

Classic Cilantro Guacamole

Total time: 15 minutes

1 avocado, halved and pitted Juice of ½ - 1 lime

¼ cup tomatoes, diced

2 tbsp cilantro, chopped

½ clove garlic

1.   Scoop out the flesh from the avocado and add as much lime juice as is needed for flavor. Mash together.

2.   Add the tomatoes, cilantro and the garlic and gently mix.

(This mixture can be blended in a food processor or blender for a smoother texture.)

Serving suggestion:

Best served with accompanying steamed broccoli florets or another cruciferous vegetable of your choice. Make sure to put some horseradish or mustard on these to "unlock" the sulforaphane content.

Gluco-raphanin	Sulfora-phane	Vitamin C	Vitamin E	β-Carotene	Omega 3	Ginger	Magnesium
		X	X	X	X		X

Week 2

Day 8

Supplements	Needed Today?
GINGER	YES
SULFORAPHANE	NO

Horseradish & Herb Dressing

Total time: 5 minutes

2 tbsp oil (refer to the table on page 34 for oil suggestions)

1 tbsp apple cider vinegar

1 tsp flat-leaf parsley, minced 1 tsp horseradish

1 tsp shallots, minced

1.   Combine all the ingredients in a food processor or blender and blend until smooth. If using a food processor, add the oil slowly as the food processor runs.

Serving suggestion:

For ultimate bioavailability, serve this dressing with cruciferous vegetables—preferably broccoli or cauliflower.

Gluco-raphanin	Sulfora-phane	Vitamin C	Vitamin E	β-Carotene	Omega 3	Ginger	Magnesium
X	X	X		X	X		

Creamy Curry Sauce

Total time: 5 minutes

4 tbsp plain yogurt

½ tsp curry powder 1 tsp lemon juice

2 tbsp oil (refer to the table on page 34 for oil suggestions)

2 tbsp fresh cilantro, chopped

1. Combine all the ingredients in a food processor or blender and blend until smooth. If using a food processor, add the oil slowly as the food processor runs.

Serving suggestion: 1 tsp of fresh ginger can be added to this dressing. It will alter the taste. But if you don't have access to supplements, if you don't want to drink ginger tea, or if you just want to bump up your ginger quota for the day, this can be an option.

* If you can, take sulforaphane supplements, even if there are cruciferous vegetables in the recipe or serving suggestion.

Gluco-raphanin	Sulfora-phane	Vitamin C	Vitamin E	β-Carotene	Omega 3	Ginger	Magnesium
		X	X		X		X

Day 9

Supplements	Needed Today?
GINGER	NO
SULFORAPHANE	NO

Ginger Almond Dressing

Total time: 5 minutes

3 tbsp almond butter

1 tbsp oil (refer to the table on page 34 for oil suggestions)

1 tbsp apple cider vinegar 1 tsp fresh ginger, grated

⅛ tsp garlic, grated 1 tbsp water

1. Combine all the ingredients in a food processor or blender and blend until smooth. If using a food processor, add the oil slowly as the food processor runs.

Serving suggestion: No specific requirements with this dressing. Pair with a meal of your choosing.

Gluco-raphanin	Sulfora-phane	Vitamin C	Vitamin E	β-Carotene	Omega 3	Ginger	Magnesium
			x		x	x	x

Simple Mustard Dressing

Total time: 5 minutes

¼ cup yogurt

2 tbsp oil (refer to the table on page 34 for oil suggestions)

2 tbsp mustard

1 tbsp lemon juice

½ clove garlic

1.   Combine all the ingredients in a food processor or blender and blend until smooth. If using a food processor, add the oil slowly as the food processor runs.

Serving suggestion: The mustard in this dressing makes it perfect for serving with cruciferous vegetables—preferably broccoli or cauliflower.

*   If you can, take sulforaphane supplements, even if there are cruciferous vegetables in the recipe or serving suggestion

Gluco-raphanin	Sulfora-phane	Vitamin C	Vitamin E	β-Carotene	Omega 3	Ginger	Magnesium
x	x	x			x		x

Day 10

Supplements	Needed Today?
GINGER	NO
SULFORAPHANE	NO

Avocado Kale Dressing

Total time: 5 minutes

1 small avocado

2 tbsp lemon juice

1 tbsp oil (refer to the table on page 34 for oil suggestions)

¼ cup kale

1. Combine all the ingredients in a food processor or blender and blend until smooth. If using a food processor, add the oil slowly as the food processor runs.

Serving suggestion: Add a dollop of mustard or horseradish to this dip to enhance sulforaphane bioavailability.

Gluco-raphanin	Sulfora-phane	Vitamin C	Vitamin E	β-Carotene	Omega 3	Ginger	Magnesium
X	X	X	X		X		X

Basil Ginger Dressing

Total time: 5 minutes

¼ cup basil, loosely packed 1 tbsp lemon juice

1 tsp fresh ginger, minced

2 tbsp oil (refer to the table on page 34 for oil suggestions)

¼ clove garlic

1.   Combine all the ingredients in a food processor or blender and blend until smooth. If using a food processor, add the oil slowly as the food processor runs.

Serving suggestion: Today all the Diabetes Reversing 8 are covered. You can be very flexible with the rest of your diet.

*   If you can, take sulforaphane supplements, even if there are cruciferous vegetables in the recipe or serving suggestion.

Gluco-raphanin	Sulfora-phane	Vitamin C	Vitamin E	β-Carotene	Omega 3	Ginger	Magnesium
				X	X	X	X

Day 11

Supplements	Needed Today?
GINGER	YES
SULFORAPHANE	NO

Lemon Arugula Dressing

Total time: 5 minutes

½ cup arugula, loosely packed 1 tbsp lemon juice

½ tsp mustard

2 tbsp oil (refer to the table on page 34 for oil suggestions)

1 tsp shallot, finely chopped

1. Combine all the ingredients in a food processor or blender and blend until smooth. If using a food processor, add the oil slowly as the food processor runs.

Serving suggestion: 1 tsp of fresh ginger can be added to this dressing. It will alter the taste. But if you don't have access to supplements, if you don't want to drink ginger tea, or if you just want to bump up your ginger quota for the day, this can be an option.

Gluco-raphanin	Sulfora-phane	Vitamin C	Vitamin E	β-Carotene	Omega 3	Ginger	Magnesium
X	X	X			X		

Red Almond Dip

Total time: 5 minutes

1 large red bell pepper 2 tbsp mustard

12 almonds

1-3 tbsp oil (refer to the table on page 34 for oil suggestions)

1.   Place almonds in a bowl of water overnight to soak and soften. If you are short on time they can be submerged in boiling water for 3-4 minutes, or if you really don't have time, they can be thrown in a food processor as they are (but more oil may be needed if the almonds are dry and you won't be getting the full nutritional potential of the almonds if you don't soak them.)

2.   Combine all the ingredients in a food processor or blender and blend until smooth. If using a food processor, add the oil slowly as the food processor runs.

Serving suggestion: You could serve broccoli with this dip, however with arugula in the earlier dressing and plenty of mustard today, it's your call if you want an extra helping of broccoli too.

*   If you can, take sulforaphane supplements, even if there are cruciferous vegetables in the recipe or serving suggestion.

Gluco-raphanin	Sulfora-phane	Vitamin C	Vitamin E	β-Carotene	Omega 3	Ginger	Magnesium
		X	X	X	X		X

Day 12

Supplements	Needed Today?
GINGER	YES
SULFORAPHANE	NO

Brocco-mole

Total time: 10 minutes

1 avocado

½ cup broccoli, no stems and finely chopped 1 tsp lemon juice

Handful fresh cilantro

½ garlic clove

1 tomato, diced (optional)

1. Mix all the ingredients together (the broccoli should be easy to mix, even though it is raw, since there are no stems and it is finely chopped.) This can be mixed by hand or in a food processor/blender. If you want a chunky brocco-mole mix by hand.

Serving suggestion: Add a dollop of mustard or horseradish to this dip if you want to enhance sulforaphane bioavailability.

Gluco-raphanin	Sulfora-phane	Vitamin C	Vitamin E	β-Carotene	Omega 3	Ginger	Magnesium
X	X	X	X				X

Spinach Basil Pesto

Total time: 10 minutes

3 tbsp spinach, chopped

2 tbsp fresh basil, chopped

1 tbsp parmesan cheese, grated

2 tbsp oil (refer to the table on page 34 for oil suggestions)

1.   Blend all the ingredients together in a food processor until almost smooth.

2.   Drizzle the oil into the mixture slowly until it is well combined.

Serving suggestion: 1 tsp of fresh ginger can be added to this dressing. It will alter the taste. But if you don't have access to supplements, if you don't want to drink ginger tea, or if you just want to bump up your ginger quota for the day, this can be an option.

*   If you can, take sulforaphane supplements, even if there are cruciferous vegetables in the recipe or serving suggestion.

Gluco-raphanin	Sulfora-phane	Vitamin C	Vitamin E	β-Carotene	Omega 3	Ginger	Magnesium
		X		X	X		X

Day 13

Supplements	Needed Today?
GINGER	NO
SULFORAPHANE	NO

Ginger Turmeric Dressing

Total time: 5 minutes

1 ½ tbsp oil (refer to the table on page 34 for oil suggestions)

1 ½ tsp mustard seeds (can be replaced with same amount of bottled mustard)

1 ½ tsp fresh ginger, grated

½ tsp fresh turmeric, grated 1 tsp lemon juice

1.   Combine all the ingredients in a food processor or blender and blend until smooth. If using a food processor, add the oil slowly as the food processor runs.

Serving suggestion: This is the perfect dressing for cauliflower. The "neutral" flavor of the cauliflower is enriched with the flavors in the dressing, not to mention given a sulforaphane boost.

Gluco-raphanin	Sulfora-phane	Vitamin C	Vitamin E	β-Carotene	Omega 3	Ginger	Magnesium
x	x	x			x	x	

Almond Basil Dip

Total time: 5 minutes

1 cup almonds

3 tbsp basil, chopped 1 tbsp lemon juice

1 tbsp oil (refer to the table on page 34 for oil suggestions)

1.   Place almonds in a bowl of water overnight to soak and soften. If you are short on time they can be submerged in boiling water for 3-4 minutes, or if you really don't have time, they can be thrown in a food processor as they are (but more oil may be needed if the almonds are dry and you won't be getting the full nutritional potential of the almonds if you don't soak them.)

2.   Combine all the ingredients in a food processor or blender and blend until smooth. If using a

food processor, add the oil slowly as the food processor runs.

Serving suggestion: No requirements for this dip.

*   If you can, take sulforaphane supplements, even if there are cruciferous vegetables in the recipe or serving suggestion.

Gluco-raphanin	Sulfora-phane	Vitamin C	Vitamin E	β-Carotene	Omega 3	Ginger	Magnesium
		X	X	X	X		X

Day 14

Supplements	Needed Today?
GINGER	YES
SULFORAPHANE	NO

Red Pepper Dressing

Total time: 10 minutes

¼ cup red bell pepper

1 tbsp oil (refer to the table on page 34 for oil suggestions)

1 tsp lemon juice

¼ clove garlic

1. Combine all the ingredients in a food processor or blender and blend until smooth. If using a food processor, add the oil slowly as the food processor runs.

Serving suggestion: 1 tsp of fresh ginger can be added to this dressing. It will alter the taste. But if you don't have access to supplements, if you don't want to drink ginger tea, or if you just want to bump up your ginger quota for the day, this can be an option.

Gluco-raphanin	Sulfora-phane	Vitamin C	Vitamin E	β-Carotene	Omega 3	Ginger	Magnesium
		X		X	X		

Spicy Avocado Dressing

Total time: 5 minutes

1 avocado

¼ cup arugula, chopped Juice of ½ lime

2 tbsp oil (refer to the table on page 34 for oil suggestions

1.   Combine all the ingredients in a food processor or blender and blend until smooth. If using a food processor, add the oil slowly as the food processor runs.

Serving Suggestion: Although mustard is not included in this recipe it is a natural pairing with any cruciferous vegetable on this protocol. You can either add it to this dressing (since arugula is high in sulforaphane) or have it with a separate serving of broccoli.

*   If you can, take sulforaphane supplements, even if there are cruciferous vegetables in the recipe or serving suggestion.

Week 3

Day 15

Supplements	Needed Today?
GINGER	NO
SULFORAPHANE	NO

Edamame Ginger Dip

Total time: 5 minutes

½ cup edamame beans (can substitute with petite peas)

½ cup arugula

1 tbsp lemon juice

½ tsp fresh ginger, grated

1.   Put all the ingredients in a blender and process until smooth.

2.   Stop the machine as needed to scrape down the sides and continue to blend until all the ingredients are liquidized.

Serving suggestion: A dollop of mustard can be added to this dip or to a side dish of cruciferous vegetables.

Gluco-raphanin	Sulfora-phane	Vitamin C	Vitamin E	β-Carotene	Omega 3	Ginger	Magnesium
X	X	X				X	X

Italian Herb Dressing

Total time: 5 minutes

¼ cup flat-leaf parsley, chopped 2 basil leaves

⅛ tsp oregano, dried

3 tbsp oil (refer to the table on page 34 for oil suggestions)

1 tbsp apple cider vinegar

¼ clove garlic

1.   Combine all the ingredients in a food processor or blender and blend until smooth. If using a food processor, add the oil slowly as the food processor runs.

Serving suggestion: There are no set requirements for this dressing. Enjoy with a meal of your choosing.

*   If you can, take sulforaphane supplements, even if there are cruciferous vegetables in the recipe or serving suggestion.

Gluco-raphanin	Sulfora-phane	Vitamin C	Vitamin E	β-Carotene	Omega 3	Ginger	Magnesium
			X	X	X		X

Day 16

Supplements	Needed Today?
GINGER	NO
SULFORAPHANE	NO

Ginger Avocado Sauce

Total time: 10 minutes

1 tbsp fresh ginger 1 avocado

1 tbsp lemon juice

1 tbsp oil (refer to the table on page 34 for oil suggestions)

1. Put ginger in the food processor and pulse till finely chopped. The remaining ingredients may then be added, and blended, until the desired consistency is reached. If this is too thick, add up to ½ cup water and/or oil.

Serving suggestion: No set requirements with this sauce. Pair with anything else you choose.

* If you can, take sulforaphane supplements, even if there are cruciferous vegetables in the recipe or serving suggestion.

Gluco-raphanin	Sulfora-phane	Vitamin C	Vitamin E	β-Carotene	Omega 3	Ginger	Magnesium
		X	X		X	X	X

Cauliflower Dressing

Total time: 5 minutes

1 ½ tsp oil (refer to the table on page 34 for oil suggestions)

1 ½ tsp lemon juice

1 ½ tsp whole grain mustard 1 ½ tsp dijon mustard

½ clove garlic, minced

1.   Combine all the ingredients in a food processor or blender and blend until smooth. If using a food processor, add the oil slowly as the food processor runs.

Serving suggestion: This dressing is really made for cauliflower. In fact, cauliflower could have been added as the 6th ingredient in this recipe, but we figure you would rather eat cauliflower than drink it. Some lightly steamed cauliflower is perfect for this flavorful dressing. Any time mustard or horseradish is in a dressing, make the most of it and pair it with cruciferous vegetables.

Gluco-raphanin	Sulfora-phane	Vitamin C	Vitamin E	β-Carotene	Omega 3	Ginger	Magnesium
X	X	X			X		

Day 17

Supplements	Needed Today?
GINGER	YES
SULFORAPHANE	NO

Creamy Avocado Sauce

Total time: 5 minutes

¼ avocado, peeled and sliced (pit removed) 2 tbsp plain yogurt

1 tbsp fresh cilantro, chopped

1   tsp flat-leaf parsley, chopped

A squeeze of lime or lemon juice

1. Add all the ingredients to a blender or food processor and mix until smooth.

Serving suggestion: 1 tsp of fresh ginger can be added to this dressing. It will alter the taste. But if you don't have access to supplements, if you don't want to drink ginger tea, or if you just want to bump up your ginger quota for the day, this can be an option.

Gluco-raphanin	Sulfora-phane	Vitamin C	Vitamin E	β-Carotene	Omega 3	Ginger	Magnesium
		X	X				X

Horseradish Dressing

Total time: 5-10 minutes

2 tbsp freshly grated horseradish (adjust according to it's strength)

¼ cup oil (refer to the table on page 34 for oil suggestions)

½ avocado

1 ¼ tbsp lemon juice

1.   Combine all the ingredients in a food processor or blender and blend until smooth. If using a food processor, add the oil slowly as the food processor runs.

Serving suggestion:

Combine with sulforaphane-rich vegetables such as broccoli or cauliflower.

*   If you can, take sulforaphane supplements, even if there are cruciferous vegetables in the recipe or serving suggestion.

Gluco-raphanin	Sulfora-phane	Vitamin C	Vitamin E	β-Carotene	Omega 3	Ginger	Magnesium
x	x	x	x		x		x

Day 18

Supplements	Needed Today?
GINGER	NO
SULFORAPHANE	NO

Spiced Lemon Dressing

Total time: 5 minutes

1 tbsp lemon juice

1 tsp fresh ginger, grated 1 tsp soy sauce

2 tbsp water

3 tbsp oil (refer to the table on page 34 for oil suggestions)

1.   Combine all the ingredients in a food processor or blender and blend until smooth. If using a food processor, add the oil slowly as the food processor runs.

Serving suggestion: No set requirements with this dressing. Pair with anything else you choose.

*   If you can, take sulforaphane supplements, even if there are cruciferous vegetables in the recipe or serving suggestion.

Gluco-raphanin	Sulfora-phane	Vitamin C	Vitamin E	β-Carotene	Omega 3	Ginger	Magnesium
		X	X		X	X	

Green Lemon Vinaigrette

Total time: 10 minutes

1 tbsp basil, chopped 1 tsp mustard

1 tsp lemon juice

3 tbsp oil (refer to the table on page 34 for oil suggestions)

¼ clove garlic, finely chopped

1.   Combine all the ingredients in a food processor or blender and blend until smooth. If using a food processor, add the oil slowly as the food processor runs.

Serving suggestion: This vinaigrette is the perfect match for a serving of cruciferous vegetables—preferably broccoli or cauliflower. The mustard makes it a natural and effective combination.

Gluco-raphanin	Sulfora-phane	Vitamin C	Vitamin E	β-Carotene	Omega 3	Ginger	Magnesium
X	X	X		X	X		X

Day 19

Supplements	Needed Today?
GINGER	NO
SULFORAPHANE	NO

Mint Ginger Dressing

Total time: 5 minutes

2 tbsp plain yogurt

1 tbsp oil (refer to the table on page 34 for oil suggestions)

½ tsp fresh ginger, grated

½ tsp fresh mint, thinly chopped

¼ tsp apple cider vinegar

1.   Combine all the ingredients in a food processor or blender and blend until smooth. If using a food processor, add the oil slowly as the food processor runs.

Serving suggestion: No set requirements with this dressing. Pair with whatever you like.

Gluco-raphanin	Sulfora-phane	Vitamin C	Vitamin E	β-Carotene	Omega 3	Ginger	Magnesium
		X			X	X	X

Horseradish Dill Sauce

Total time: 10 minutes

3 tbsp plain yogurt 2 tsp onion, grated

1 tbsp oil (refer to the table on page 34 for oil suggestions)

½ tsp lemon juice (can add more if you like)

½ tsp horseradish

½ tsp dill weed, chopped

1. Combine all the ingredients in a food processor or blender and blend until smooth. If using a food processor, add the oil slowly as the food processor runs.

Serving suggestion: This goes especially well with fish. Also, make sure you utilize the power of horseradish and pair with a sulforaphane-rich vegetable such as broccoli or cauliflower.

*   If you can, take sulforaphane supplements, even if there are cruciferous vegetables in the recipe or serving suggestion.

Gluco-raphanin	Sulfora-phane	Vitamin C	Vitamin E	β-Carotene	Omega 3	Ginger	Magnesium
X	X	X	X		X		X

Day 20

Supplements	Needed Today?
GINGER	YES
SULFORAPHANE	NO

Mustard Lemon Dip

Prep time: 5 minutes Cook time: 5-6 minutes

½ cup kale, chopped 1 avocado

1 ½ tsp lemon juice

⅛ tsp dry mustard (can substitute for bottled mustard)

1 tsp oil (refer to the table on page 34 for oil suggestions)

1.   Add the kale to the frying pan with some oil and cook over a medium-low heat. Stir the kale occasionally, until it wilts and becomes tender (approx. 5-6 minutes.) When wilted, transfer to a chopping board and finely chop.

2.   Halve the avocado, remove pit and scoop out the flesh, placing it into the food processor. To this, add the lemon juice, and dry mustard. Process until smooth.

3.   In a separate bowl, transfer the avocado mixture from the food processor and mix in kale pieces by hand.

Serving suggestion: None for this dip. Serve with anything you choose. The dry mustard in this dip is already paired with sulforaphane-rich kale.

Gluco-raphanin	Sulfora-phane	Vitamin C	Vitamin E	β-Carotene	Omega 3	Ginger	Magnesium
X	X	X	X		X		X

Herbed Yogurt Dressing

Total time: 5 minutes

¼ cup plain yogurt 3 tbsp fresh parsley 1 tbsp lemon juice

½ tsp coriander, ground

¼ garlic clove

1. Place all the ingredients in a food process or blender and blend until smooth.

Serving suggestion: 1 tsp of fresh ginger can be added to this dressing. It will alter the taste. But if you don't have access to supplements, if you don't want to drink ginger tea, or if you just want to bump up your ginger quota for the day, this can be an option.

*   If you can, take sulforaphane supplements, even if there are cruciferous vegetables in the recipe or serving suggestion.

Gluco-raphanin	Sulfora-phane	Vitamin C	Vitamin E	β-Carotene	Omega 3	Ginger	Magnesium
		X		X			X

Day 21

Supplements	Needed Today?
GINGER	YES
SULFORAPHANE	NO

Almond Mint-Parsley Sauce

Total time: 5 minutes

12 almonds

½ clove garlic

1mtsp apple cider vinegar

2mtbsp oil (refer to the table on page 34 for oil suggestions)

2mtbsp fresh parsley, chopped 3 tbsp fresh mint, chopped

1.   Place almonds in a bowl of water overnight to soak and soften. If you are short on time they can be submerged in boiling water for 3-4 minutes, or if you really don't have time, they can be thrown in a food processor as they are (but more oil may be needed if the almonds are dry and you won't be getting the full nutritional potential of the almonds if you don't soak them.)

2.   Combine all the ingredients in a food processor or blender and blend until smooth. If using a food processor, add the oil slowly as the food processor runs.

Serving suggestion:

Although sulforaphane supplements aren't technically "needed" today, a single dose can be taken. Otherwise, a small serving of broccoli with some horseradish/mustard will suffice. (And I do mean small since there is kale in the following recipe.)

Gluco-raphanin	Sulfora-phane	Vitamin C	Vitamin E	β-Carotene	Omega 3	Ginger	Magnesium
		X	X	X	X		X

Kale Guacamole

Total time: 15 minutes

3mtbsp kale, blanched and chopped 2 tsp cilantro, chopped

1 ½ avocados, mashed

A squeeze of lemon juice

1.   Remove the tough stem from the kale and place the leaves in boiling water until tender

(around 45 seconds.)

2.   Following this, submerge the blanched kale in ice water until chilled. Dry the leaves and finely mince.

3.   Mash the avocados and add a squeeze of lemon juice.

4.   Mix in the kale and cilantro, until well combined.

Serving suggestion: 1 tsp of fresh ginger can be added to this dressing. It will alter the taste. But if you don't have access to supplements, if you don't want to drink ginger tea, or if you just want to bump up your ginger quota for the day, this can be an option.

Gluco-raphanin	Sulfora-phane	Vitamin C	Vitamin E	β-Carotene	Omega 3	Ginger	Magnesium
X	X	X	X				X

SUCCESS GUARANTEED

You now have everything you need to succeed with The Halki Diabetes Remedy. The real cause of diabetes has been revealed, as have the wonders behind the Diabetes Reversing 8. You have over

30 recipes containing these anti-inflammatory, anti-oxidant filled, super nutrient-dense substances and a 21 day plan to help you every step of the way.

As I stated in the beginning, my goal in writing this eBook was to give you hope, and help you see that there is light at the end of the tunnel. I am sure you have been used to living in darkness, that the idea of light might have seemed like a fantasy. I wanted this eBook to be concrete proof to you, a bible of sorts, to give you that light and pull you out from the tunnel. No more darkness. No more despair. Just a new life for you and those you love.

Remember that this isn't a complicated program, it will do what you need it to when you follow it. The only prerequisite is to have the ingredients and put them in your mouth. Always know what you're eating and when, know the protocol, and if you need to supplement with anything that day. Stick to the protocol, however, also remember that there is a certain amount of flexibility, so if you really feel like having a sweet dip rather than the savory one that was planned for the day, you can, just remember to have the entire day's dips (both of them) and follow the suggested supplementation for that day. You want to keep them in their set, not breaking the dips up randomly. They are paired together each day for a reason, and so long as you keep them together, you're good. Also remember that the lunch and dinner dips can be switched - if you feel like having one of them earlier in the day, then do. So long as you get those Diabetes Reversing 8 into your day, you're golden!

When you have completed the 21 day plan you can continue with any of the dressings or dips. They are so easy to make that I like to keep a couple ready-made in the fridge, preferably in their daily pairing. See what works for you; use them to enrich your life and promote continued good health.

WELCOME TO YOUR NEW LIFE

You may have forgotten what it was like before you had to deal with diabetes, before the worry of your health and finances and losing loved ones engulfed everything else. Now that you know the secret to changing your life, to reversing diabetes, you can step into the life you've wanted, the one waiting for you on the other side of where you are right now. You have everything you need for your amazing new, diabetes-free life. What are you waiting for?

41451622R00073

Made in the USA
San Bernardino, CA
02 July 2019